MW00955051

The 40-Day Journey

For Women

Encounter God, Discover You, Experience Freedom

Josie Muterspaw

Copyright © 2018 by Josie Muterspaw

No part of this book may be reproduced or transmitted in any form or by any means, electronic. or mechanical, including photocopying and recording, or by any information storage or retrieval system without the express written permission of the publisher.

All Scripture quotations, unless otherwise indicated, are taken from the Holy Bible, New Living Translations, NLT, © 1996, 2013,2015 by Tyndale House Publishers, Inc. Used by permission of Tyndale House Publishers, Inc. Carol Stream, Illinois 60188. All rights reserved. Scripture quotation marked TPT are from The Passion Translation. Copyright © 2017by BroadStreet Publishing Group, LLC. Used by permission. All rights reserved.thePassionTranslation.com. Scripture quotation marked MSG are taken from the Holy Bible: The Message (the Bible in contemporary language). 2005. Colorado Springs, CO: NavPress. Used by permission. All Rights reserved. Scripture quotation marked ESV are taken from the ESV Bible (The Holy Bible, English Standard Version), copyright © 2001 by Crossway, a publishing ministry of Good News Publishers. Used by permission. All right reserved. Scripture quotations marked NIV are taken from The Holy Bible, New International Version, Copyright © 1973, 1978, 1984, 2011 by Biblica, Inc. Used by permission. All right reserved worldwide. Scripture quotations marked AMP are taken from the AMPLIFIED Bible, Copyright © 1954, 1958, 1962, 1964, 1965, 1987 by The Lockman Foundation. All right reserved. Used by permission. (www.Lockman.org)

Printed in the United States of America

First Printing, 2018

ISBN 9781975831868

Polishing Copy Editor Caroll L. Shreeve @ My Write Art Place

For ordering information contact:

Shine Healing Ministries

www.shinehealing.org

Contents

Introduction 6

The 40-Day Guidelines 29

Encounter God

Day 1 Expectation and Praise 31
Day 2 Your View of God 36
Day 3 God's Relentless Love 41
Day 4 God's Character 46
Day 5 God's Promises 51
Day 6 His Sacrifice—Our Freedom 56
Day 7 Hearing God's Heart 61

Discover You

Day 8 Setting the Stage—Your Family of Origin..67
Day 9 The Ups and Downs—Your Life Timeline 72
Day 10 Identifying Your Likes, Wants, and Desires 77
Day 11 Your Unique Personality Style 82
Day 12 Daily Habits and Self-Care Routines 87
Day 13 What Makes Your Heart Light Up? 92
Day 14 Your Greatest Fears 97
Day 15 How Receptive Are You? 102
Day 16 The Power of Connection 107
Day 17 Your Emotions 112
Day 18 Your Mindsets 117
Day 19 Your Protective Strategies 122
Day 20 Tucked-Away Places 127
Day 21 The Labels You've Accepted 132
Day 22 The Hope Within You 137

Experience Freedom

Day 23 Your True Identity—God's View of You...143

Day 24 Self-Forgiveness 148

Day 25 Forgiving Others 153

Day 26 Forgiving God...158

Day 27 Making Amends 163

Day 28 Breaking Free..168

Day 29 Being Made New 173

Day 30 Preparing Your Heart for R.E.S.T...178

Day 31–37 Your Unique R.E.S.T Experience..183-211

Day 38 Reflections from R.E.S.T..212

Day 39 The Light Inside You 217

Day 40 Share Your Story...222

Appendix

Next Steps—Join the 40-Day Journey Community...227

Weekly Emotions Journal 229

Common Negative Limiting Mindsets and Protective Strategies 231

Encouragement for the Road Ahead—Freedom Reminders...232

About the Author 233

Dedication & Special Thanks

To all the dreamers who have yet to realize how bright their light
can shine and to my amazing husband who has been my rock
and encourager through the process of seeing God's vision
come to life in our lives.

Introduction

"In the silence of the heart, God Speaks."

Mother Teresa

I have come to realize there is no freedom without rest. It is contrary to our regular mode of thinking, but then again, Jesus' ways have always confounded the wise. They say, "*Less is more*". When it comes to finding the freedom we all seek, this simple phrase is undeniably true. Less of us leads to more of Him (John 3:30). More of God leads to the discovery of our purpose and the courage to fulfill it!

On this 40-day journey set before you, my prayer is that you will learn to recognize the rhythm of God's heartbeat and experience the peace that comes from resting in God's way as you learn to cease from yours. God is waiting. He can't wait for you to open your heart fully before him so that he can lead you on the path to the "immeasurably more" he has planned for your life (Ephesians 3:20).

There is a desire in all of us to know who we were created to be, and it burns within us to fulfill it. I'm convinced that the greatest source of discontentment spills out of a heart that doesn't know its purpose! For we have been created by a God who thought about us before we were even born and set us apart for a uniquely designed destiny (Jeremiah 1:5). The questions, "Who am I?" and "Why am I here?", can only be answered when we pause to seek the One who knows. God formed you, and designed every part of you and he can't wait to whisper in your ear who you are!

The 40-Day Journey

The 40-Day Journey is your next step guide created from the principles discussed in my book, *Shining Freely,* and is designed to assist you with putting into practice what you have learned. Through the process of writing *Shining Freely,* I sought to discover God's design for healing in our lives. But it wasn't until I came to the last chapter that I realized where the answer to all freedom lies. Being fully free to shine our lights without hindrance, only comes through rest! As you learn to rest in God's presence, he will free your soul and empower your every step. Let *The 40-Day Journey* guide you into an experience with God's heart that will blow you away. Your part in this process is to allow yourself to experience something new. Even if it means letting go of the beliefs and strategies you've always trusted.

This journey you are about to travel is not just meant to last 40 days. No, my goal is that your experience will lead to a lifestyle change. A lifestyle of dependence on God as your new and improved GPS system. This experience is designed to teach you the *Art of the Pause*—pausing, waiting, and resting in God's presence. It is an intentional practice of pausing from life to hear God's heart without distractions or fear. For it is in the stillness of his presence that our hearts become free to see who we really are. Then nestled in his heart peace fills the space, and we find the courage to run after his vision for our lives.

David beautifully paints this path to restoration and purpose for us in Psalm 23: 2–3 (TPT) when he describes God's rest:

> He offers a resting place for me in his luxurious love. His tracks take me to an oasis of peace, the quiet brook of bliss. That's where he restores and revives my life. He opens before me pathways to God's pleasure and leads me along in his footsteps of righteousness so that I can bring honor to his name.

God is offering us a resting place beside him surrounded by his love. An offering means we have to receive it and allow ourselves to experience it. As we open our hearts, he will lead us to an "oasis of peace" far away from the distractions of this world. That is where he will restore and revive our weary souls. It is only when he knows we are ready—fully infused with his strength, power, and presence that he will illuminate before us the path that he has designed for our lives. Then full of his presence, we honor him. Spilling over, we spread the sweet fragrance of his presence everywhere we go.

His presence is where our freedom lies, our hearts come alive, and our purposes are set free! Dare to take this journey with me and encounter God in a whole new way. Let him show you who you are so that you can experience the freedom to be all he has created you to be!

Rest Is About Ceasing

The type of "Rest" we are learning to do along this 40-day journey is from ourselves—ceasing from our ingrained ways of perceiving and reacting! You will discover things about yourself on this journey that are holding you back. Most often it is the *beliefs* we hold that produce behaviors that align our lives with limiting outcomes. The psalmist proclaimed, "I'm single-minded in pursuit of you" (Psalms 119:10, MSG). Ceasing is an intentional practice of laying down what you have always done and always believed to be "single-minded" in the pursuit of what God has for you each day.

We simply must stop doing life our own way and learn to cease from *our work* so that God can finally do *his work* in our lives! Jesus said:

> Are you weary, carrying a heavy burden? Then come to me. I will refresh your life, for I am your oasis. Simply join your life with mine. Learn my ways and you'll discover that I'm gentle, humble, easy to please. You will find refreshment and rest in me (Matthew 11:28-30, TPT).

Rest is his gift to us. Jesus is asking us to give him the burdens we have placed on ourselves, so he can set us free. He longs for us to come and drink of him and promises that if we do, he will be our *oasis* and refresh our dry and weary places. The definition and synonyms of oasis paint a vibrant picture of what Jesus is wanting to be for us when we are weighed down by the burdens of this life. When he says, "I am your oasis," he is wanting you to see that he is your: watering place, your peace, your retreat, your sanctuary, your shelter, your harbor, your refuge, your relief, your restorer, your pleasant change, your sustenance, your safe place, your haven, your nourishment, your place of growth, your covering, your hideaway, your resting place, your escape, your well, your spring, and your ever-flowing fountain. Join with him, learn his ways, and let him be your oasis.

This rest Jesus offers us is largely misunderstood in our culture today. Bible teachers, Graham Cooke and Priscilla Shirer, both heavily influenced my understanding of rest as God designed it. They opened my eyes to this amazing gift God was asking me to receive. Here are a few of the truths I discovered about REST that completely redefined my view:

- Rest is the path to freedom
- Rest is a weapon—our spiritual armor
- Rest is a lifestyle created by God for us to enjoy
- Rest is God's mercy
- Rest is where peace flows from
- Rest uproots the old and plants anew
- Rest releases the burdens we've placed on ourselves
- Rest is where God prepares us for who we are to be
- Rest is the birth place of God-size dreams
- Rest accelerates healing
- Rest is the source of God's revelation and wisdom
- Rest is God's gift to us
- Rest breaks chains and slavery mindsets
- Rest guards our hearts, keeping us from slipping back into old areas of bondage
- Rest cements truth
- Rest breeds miracles
- Rest refocuses our attention on what matters most
- Rest ignites hope and inspires vision

Rest doesn't sound so bad now does it? The busy pace of our culture makes us see rest (ceasing, pausing) as something wrong for us to do. Yet, it is God's design for us to learn to rest in and rely on him. The enemy will plant thought after thought in your mind making rest seem insignificant, impossible, or irresponsible with the intent on keeping you from experiencing the freedom that only results from a place of rest!

As a clinical counselor, specializing in the treatment of trauma, I've seen the trend. When looking back at the clients I have had who remained in the wilderness of their pain and were unable to cross over into their "promised land" of healing, they all had a common denominator. They struggled to *cease* in one area or another. Painful experiences had caused their fear to grow and their trust to dwindle. They had limiting mindsets they fought hard to hold onto, self-protective strategies they refused to let go of, and unforgiveness that stood guard at the gate to their hearts. It makes sense. It is not an easy task to let go of all we've known and what we believe protects us to embrace something that feels uncertain and foreign.

Priscilla Shirer, points out an undeniable truth that, "Recognition is the prerequisite of liberation." We must realize, we can't avoid forever and heal. There are consequences that result from not letting go of things we were never meant to hold. Our freedom is at stake! Freedom comes when we find the courage to look at the things we are believing and the strategies we have devised that result in being chained to the very things we want to be free from. When we cease from ourselves and allow God's truth to guide our hearts, he will use our obedience to usher in a healing wave of freedom and accelerate the plans he has had for us all along!

What Am I Asking You to Do?

Learning to pause in God's presence and hear his heart is the single most important thing you will ever do in this life. *The 40-Day Journey* guides you each day into taking actions that lead you to encounter God in a whole new way and R.E.S.T in him. The journey I am asking you to walk will involve:

Relaxing your hold of the reins and ceasing from your self-protective strategies

Escaping from your limiting mindsets by aligning your view with God's Word

Starting a lifestyle of dependence and trust in *who* God is for you

SO THAT YOU CAN...

Triumph over any obstacle attempting to block you from experiencing the freedom to live out your purpose!

How Do We Learn to Cease So That God Can Begin?

As I have already alluded to, we learn to rest in God's way by ceasing from ourselves. Each day on *The 40-Day Journey* you will be practicing the art of the pause as I guide you in the principles of ceasing. To C.E.A.S.E means to choose each day to:

Connect with the one true source of all healing. God alone is our healer! Connecting vertically is a must before anything can change horizontally. Each day of this journey begins with meditating on a scripture verse and preparing your heart to experience God's view of you and the miracles he wants to do in you through worship.

Examine your heart. This is your time to be honest and real with yourself and God. Let God bring awareness to the things in your heart that he wants to free you from. This step is about asking yourself the tough questions you would rather avoid. Be willing to look at the thoughts you are believing and things you are doing that are creating a lack of freedom in the areas of your life highlighted in each day.

Allow God to give you his view by seeking his perspective. During this step try to visualize what God is speaking into your heart and put yourself in the scene of his grace. Always use God's Word as your litmus test for any thought that enters your mind during this process and guard what you allow to have access to your heart. We can easily accept false beliefs into our heart and be led away from truth. We must fight to discover what God wants us to believe instead and allow his truth to become our sole focus.

Surrender your way for God's Way. This step is about aligning our hearts and minds with the truth God reveals. Here we let go of and repent of anything we've been believing or doing that keeps God's truth from entering our hearts and producing fruit in our lives. A repentant heart is a freed heart! When we repent of the things that don't line up with God's truth, we break the power they hold over us. God never intended for repentance to make us feel condemned or shameful. No, he asks us to repent so that we can experience freedom. He wants us to let go of what we were never meant to hold, so that he can open our hearts to what we were designed to experience—his grace! As you let go and turn to God, it allows him to fill you with his love and grace and literally cut the ties to the limiting mindsets, protective strategies, and unhealthy bonds in your life.

Expect God to show up for you. Believe that he will be faithful to complete the work he began in you (Philippians 1:6). Praise him for the changes coming and open your eyes to what he has already done. Encourage your heart by renewing your mind in the truth God reveals to you each day and remember to stay free by guarding what you allow access to your heart and mind. Choose to focus your mind on his truth and speak it out loud over your life, and don't forget to record where you see God moving in your life as you practice ceasing from your way to surrender to his (Deuteronomy 4:9).

Two Bonus Sections

Pause, Sit and Soak In His Presence

We are changed through relational encounters with God. As we practice taking our eyes off the circumstance and focusing instead on who God is trying to be for us in our struggle, we can begin to experience the peace his presence always brings. This space is meant to encourage you to spend time connecting with the greatest encourager of all. God wants to deepen the truth he will highlight in your heart each today through creativity. He wants to move your heart in ways that light up his path for your life! Worship leader, Jeremy Riddle, says, "Creativity holds keys to our identity". God will use his unlimited creativity to help you envision yourself as he sees you! So I challenge you, even if you are not artistically inclined, to allow God's creative nature to flow in your heart and express what is bubbling up inside you in fun and inspirational ways!

Mining Deeper

This is truly my favorite section. This space is where you record your adventures seeking and mining for the treasures in God's heart. As you continue to seek God for answers to your heart's questions, he will begin to reveal to you in multiple ways over the course of weeks, months and even years revelations that will blow you away and encourage the deepest parts of your soul. He is faithful to continually place things in front of you that reassure you and help you experience deeper levels of freedom. Daniel 2:22 tells us that God reveals deep and hidden things. God loves when we dig deep into his presence and seek his heart. He has so much he wants to show us. He wants us to discover more about how he sees us, how he views our situation, and who he wants to be for us in the process. There are hidden treasures yet to be discovered and God can't wait to reveal them to you!

Why 40 days?

Quite simply because we need intentional focus and repetition in order to change our old habits and stop doing what we've always done. Biblically, the number forty often represents a long journey or significant time period. It is the number of testing, trial, and wilderness on one end and deliverance, transformation, and triumph on the other. We dread these seemingly harsh and dry seasons, yet it is in the wilderness or "paused" moments of our lives where God's presence can be experienced, and transformation can begin.

I must, however, point out that there is a key to this journey that will unlock even greater levels of transformation and freedom in your life. It is your obedience. Your will. Your ability to choose whether or not you will let go of what God asks you to release during this journey. It's true, God will ask some things of you that seem impossible. Your task is to learn to trust in his goodness. If he is asking you to let it go, it is because it is holding you back from receiving all he wants to give you. Let your heart rely on him to guide you every step of the way (Proverbs 3:5). For in the end, your obedience in the "40" will determine your outcome.

Moses is a notable example of obedience. His 40 years in the wilderness prepared his heart to trust God when he was asked to do the impossible. God spoke to him through a burning bush and told a known stutter to speak before Pharaoh and release his people. Moses was tempted to say no and he even tried to convince God that he must have chosen the wrong person, but we know how the story ends. Moses' journey of inner transformation was completed by his obedience. The result, an unheard-of number of people were rescued from Egyptian oppression as the Red Sea parted before them.

Moses experienced the miracles God wanted to do through him because he had developed a practice of slipping away to be alone in God's presence. Just months after entering the wilderness, Moses spent 40 days on Mount Sinai interceding for his people and seeking God's instructions for the journey ahead. Exodus 34 tells the story of how he came back down the mountain radiant with God's presence holding the Ten commandments. These were the instructions the people needed in order for them to live and thrive as the freed people they now were. God knew his people wouldn't survive in this uncharted territory if they remained in their old ways. They needed new instructions, new habits, new mindsets in order for them to take hold of all he had promised.

I wonder what it was like for Moses to walk down from that mountain-top encounter glowing with God's presence and holding in his hands the Ten Commandments that he saw being inscribed before him by the very finger of God. Could you image that? Moses' 40 days alone with God, forever changed history. That's what God can do when we are obedient in the 40. He floods our hearts with his light and reveals to us truth that forever changes us and molds us into the difference makers we are designed to be.

Jesus is another example of being obedient in the 40. He overcame the greatest temptation of his life after spending 40 days alone with his Father in the wilderness. God was preparing him to save the entire world from sin, death, and captivity. Even Jesus, when faced with such a task cried out to his father and said, "If it is possible, let this cup of suffering be taken from me. Yet I want your will to be done, not mine" (Matthew 26:39, NLT). In the end, his obedience lead to the greatest rescue mission that ever was and ever will be by dying on the Cross so that every human heart can experience freedom.

A Journey of Faithfulness

Faith is what allows our hearts to capture what our eyes can't see. Faith encourages our feet to leap when our minds say, "There's no way". As I sought to fully grasp the significance of this journey, I realized that this is a journey of faithfulness. It is where we learn to become unwavering, steady, and reliable people of the promise. If we are honest, if God were to give us right now everything we ask of him, would we be unwavering, and reliable? Would we be willing to do whatever he asks of us to fulfill it? This journey will require us to takes steps that make our legs wobbly and our hearts beat wildly. Will we learn to be people who are willing to put one foot in front of the other trusting God to lead the way no matter what he asks of us?

This is our chance to refuse to give up, give in, or back down and become people who learn to let go of "...every wound that has pierced us" and everything that weighs us down. It is where we learn to truly run—run with the determination to finish the race God has pre-destined and marked out for us (Hebrews 12:1, TPT).

We learn to be faithful and obedient in the space between the promise God makes to us and the capture of it. It all comes down to what happens in the middle. I used to believe it was about getting to the destination, but God helped me to realize, no, it is all about the transformation. The inner transformation that takes place as we become the person that can capture the promise God has given us and run with it with all our might.

For both Jesus and Moses, obedience in the 40 led to results only God could produce. The Israelites, however, are proof of promises unfulfilled when obedience and faithfulness are lacking. None of the original crew rescued from Egypt, entered the promised land after 40 years in the wilderness. They were right there. They saw it with their own eyes and even tasted of its fruit. They had a promise from God that the land was theirs, but they couldn't see past the obstacles. They never let the journey transform them into people who believed they could capture the promise.

In Numbers 13, Moses sent out the spies to scope out the land God had already promised was theirs for the taking. After 40 days of scouting, only two came back with a positive report. Only two let faith lead the way. Caleb and Joshua saw from their hearts not their eyes and focused on God's words not the giants ahead of them. The Israelites heard the promises of God and saw it with their own eyes, but they allowed the fear of what they couldn't do overpower their trust in what only God could accomplish. The result, they remained chained to the past and unable to walk into the land that overflowed with God's provision and purpose.

Hundreds of years later, the Israelites once again found themselves in a similar conundrum. This time the giant, Goliath, taunted an entire army of warriors for 40 days. Every morning he would intimidate them with lies that they believed, paralyzing them so that they could not advance. Until one day, David, a mere shepherd boy who let his experience of God lead his vision, took down the giant and saved an entire nation.

Be ready for the giant. He will surely show up throughout your 40-day journey as well. Especially at the end, just when you are about to cross over into new levels of freedom. He will increase the taunting, trying his best to paralyze you and stop you from advancing into what is yours for the taking! The enemy taunts you, spouting lies because he is terrified you will realize who you are in Christ. He knows he can't keep God from making you a promise, but if he can get you to believe his lies, he can keep you from allowing God to transform you into the person who can fulfill it. Your life was meant to impact others for the kingdom. Don't let the giants in your way make you lose sight of the fact that you were made for more! Keep your eyes fixed and focused on God's Word and his promises. Then you will see your giants fall!

What Exactly Are We Ceasing From?
Negative Limiting Mindsets

First and foremost, we have to discover what we are constantly saying to ourselves and bring awareness to the thoughts that replay in our minds. Our beliefs shape who we become, and our experiences create our perceptions. The problem is, sometimes these perceptions lead us far from the truth. Therefore, it is vital that we learn to recognize what beliefs we have formed in our minds when overwhelmed in our hearts; because these beliefs can turn into rigid mindsets that end up paralyzing our destinies. I chose the word "mindset" because it means a "fixed state of mind or an inclination" (Merriam Webster). To me, "*fixed*", feels like a mind made up, something that is hard to change, or convince otherwise. Which explains why it is so hard to change a belief once it has been ingrained.

Perhaps because of early life experiences you have formed limiting mindsets such as: "I don't deserve love," "I am stupid," "I am worthless," "I am a failure," "Everything is my fault," "I have no control," "I am permanently damaged," "I am powerless to change anything," "I cannot trust myself," "I'm bad," "I'm not safe—people will always hurt me," "I can't trust anyone". The list can go on and on. What we tell ourselves becomes our truth. *The 40-Day Journey* is about fixing our heart on God's truth instead so that our lives begin to align with how he sees us!

Self-Protective Strategies

The second thing we are learning to cease from on this journey is our self-protective strategies. Negative limiting mindsets lead to the creation of self-directed (not God-directed) strategies. When we experience the hurt of a broken heart, we naturally want to protect ourselves from ever feeling that way again. So, we make silent promises to ourselves and devise strategies (often unconscious) to ensure our own protection. It may sound a little something like this, "I'll never_____" (fill in the blank). This promise turns into a self-protective strategy to protect our hearts from experiencing more hurt.

For example, you may have promised yourself to never trust anyone ever again because you were hurt by those who were supposed to protect you most. This promise turns into a self-protective strategy of self-reliance and causes you to never ask for help from others or depend on anyone. This includes God. The result, you end up creating the very hurt you are trying to protect yourself from. Your self-protective strategy ensures the continuation of the cycle of always feeling like no one is ever there for you because you promised yourself to never need anyone ever again!

The 40-Day Journey is about stopping this cycle of hurt in our lives and learning to depend on God so that we can experience true and lasting freedom! Hebrews 4:11 tells us to be "diligent to enter rest". It is an intentional decision we must make to rest from ourselves, so that God can break us free! It's time. Your limiting mindsets, self-promises, and protective strategies need the light of God's truth to pierce the hidden places within and transform you from the inside out. Allow God to prepare your heart for the great and mighty things he has planned for your future!

My 40-Day Journey

Obedience doesn't come easy for us. Or is it just me? Three years of pushing and striving, desperate to make happen the dream God put in my heart and still everything seemed to be falling apart. Nothing was flowing, nothing was happening. Relationships were crumbling, and the pieces just weren't falling into place. Then in the fall of 2016, God impressed on my heart to rest for 40 days. Rest! What? For 40 days? "Lord, don't you see I am trying to launch a ministry here." But then I realized, God had to be asking me to do this for a reason.

So, I tried.

I lasted twenty-five days the first time. I fell off the wagon and right back into my protective strategy of striving, doing, and pushing. You see, I had an underlying negative limiting mindset that kept tell me, "If I'm not doing, I'm nothing". All my value was resting on what I could *do* for God instead of who he already was in me!

Since I hadn't quite learned how to cease from me, I planned a strategy weekend with my team. Yep, that's right. In the middle of what was supposed to be 40 days of rest and ceasing from my way, I planned a strategy weekend. It's hard to admit, but what it really came down to was I didn't trust God to do his part, so I over-did mine! God had to be chuckling a little at this point. In my mind, dedicated time away was all that was needed to launch this new endeavor. But no matter how much I pushed, I couldn't make it happen. It wasn't that God didn't want this vision to come to pass, but the timing was off.

Time has always been my nemesis. Nothing is ever fast enough, soon enough, or checked off my list quickly enough. I should have gotten the memo when every attempt to move forward fizzled. But, no, I kept trying to pound down doors that God knew I wasn't ready to open. No movement caused frustration to brew within me. So, what did I do? You would hope I would say listen and rest. Nope. Not me. I kept pushing, ending up in a forced rest, confined to the lovely white, sterile walls of my very own hospital room.

Stress does some pretty-crazy things to our bodies. I woke up one Saturday morning, foggy and disoriented. I was struggling to form coherent thoughts and words. My eyesight suddenly changed, and the left side of my body went numb. No more excuses. Off to the hospital I went. Rounds and rounds of tests to rule out a mini stroke and possible Multiple Sclerosis (MS), stopped me in my tracks. I'm lucky. I walked out of the hospital with the label "stressed" and a bit of a bruised ego but not MS.

So, when I heard the Lord say rest the second time, I listened! It was the best decision of my life. Go figure. The three-year journey I traveled while writing my book, *Shining Freely*, and living out the concepts within it, changed me for sure, but the most accelerated change came from the 40-day gift I had been resisting. This gift allowed me to see that shining freely (being the light we were uniquely created to be without hindrance) only happens when we experience God's rest!

I realized I didn't understand true freedom because I didn't know rest. You see there was a missing piece in the healing equation I hadn't personally experienced and it wasn't until I ceased from my striving that I found the answer. All true healing and restoration comes through stillness—when we pause long enough to experience God's presence and gain his perspective!

Priscilla Shirer explains beautifully why we fail to experience true freedom. She said, "The Israelites had lived in slavery for so long that their inclination—even once outside of Egypt—was to live like they were still in bondage." She went on to say that:

> The reality is—for them and for us—that once slavery has been internalized, the mind remains in bondage even when the body is free ... God prescribed for His people—then and now—a loving, gracious gift that would break the chains that remained inside of them. The gift was called the Sabbath.

I heard it once said that you can't solve a heart issue with the mind. The problem is we are always trying to analyze and rationalize with our minds which leads us to repeat the behaviors that keep us stuck in our old ways. We have lost the art of listening with our heart. We are terrified of it really. Yet, it is only in the stillness that God can speak the very truth our hearts need to hear so that we can walk free.

We all have one—a pesky limiting mindset that holds us back. All of us struggling with our own individual versions of "not being enough". I was a slave to doing, to prove that I wasn't insignificant after all. I was believing a lie that kept me stuck in a cycle of striving, then beating myself up for not being perfect, then striving some more, until I eventually fell-down on my knees in disappointment. I repeated this cycle over an over until I finally learned to stop pushing and trust that God would lead the way.

The Israelites had their own cycle. They complained and moaned, God provided, they enjoyed his provision, then forgot what he had done, and complained and moaned again. Their lives reveal to us the devastation that can result from being physically free but never pausing to make sure our minds are free. Could it be that we too are really free, but remain captive only by our own minds?

Three Foundational Cracks

During my 40 days, God revealed three foundational cracks that he needed to be mended within me in order to bring my life back into balance. The first one was an imbalance between family and ministry. I was so driven to produce the dream of helping others heal that I was neglecting my own family. I was consumed at times and they paid the price. You can get really self-absorbed into a good thing. In rest, God renewed and strengthened my relationships within my family. He reset my eyes and I realized family was my priority, my first ministry, my greatest ministry.

The second foundational crack formed because of my imbalanced view of responsibility. This was God's dream to fulfill. I was dependent upon him, not the other way around. Embracing his power at work in me to do what I could never do relieved the pressure. I had been carrying a burden on my shoulders, trying to gain the knowledge, strength, and skills to help others heal. God was saying, "let me do that." I heard God speak to my heart, "Never underestimate the power of an encounter with me." My job was just to create the space that directed others to him and he would do the rest.

Another layer of freedom.

The third foundational crack God needed to heal in my heart was my imbalanced view of God's goodness. I couldn't understand why he wasn't providing the resources the ministry needed, and I struggled to trust in God's desire to do so. I feared lack. Priscilla called it "scarcity scared". This fear turned me into a person I didn't want to be. I began to focus my energy on ways I could bring in money instead of focusing on how the ministry could bring value to others. Living with a fear of lack caused me to resist rest because I felt like it all depended on me and worst of all, fearing lack created a generosity void in my heart.

Ouch.

I heard in my heart God say, "I will provide for the dreams I have for you. Some of the lack you feel is because you are pushing for me to come behind your dream instead of you walking out mine." The resources I was seeking were for the wrong direction. God wanted to do *a new thing* in me, but I was plowing forward with blinders on. The lack of provision was not because God did not want to provide for me, but because I was seeking provision in areas to which he was not leading.

God was healing these foundational cracks in me piece by piece. One thing that fed my push to strive harder, was my need for people's approval. I was reading from Rick Renner's *Sparkling Gems* devotional one morning and he was breaking down the original meaning of the verse in 1 Thessalonians 2:4. "We have been approved by God to be entrusted with the Gospel, so we speak not to please man, but to please God who tests our hearts." God was working on my heart so that whatever I accomplished would be motivated by pleasing him, not man. Rick said,

> It's hard on the flesh while we wait, yet it is actually God's mercy at work. He is trying to keep us from moving into a new position and falling flat on our faces because we didn't take the time to allow him to expose all the hidden flaws. During the time of waiting the imperfections that would have ruined us are exposed so God can remove them.

God knew I was headed for a fall. In his grace he swooped in and exposed my hidden flaws. It was then that I realized if I kept living for people's approval, I'd never reach the level he wanted for me. There are too many of you—it is impossible to please you all. I had to learn to be consumed by his approval alone. Best of all, God wanted me to experience his love for me whether I was performing or not. He gently whispered to my heart, "I don't love you for what you do for me, Josie. I love you for you."

I was overwhelmed by God's heart. I realized this wait; this pause in my life was all God's mercy at work! We are all broken in our own way. God asked me to stop long enough for him to mend the cracked places in me, because he knew if I pushed forward before I was ready, I would completely fall apart. He was exposing things I didn't know existed to keep me from experiencing a deeper hurt.

In Galatians 1:17, Paul mentions his season of hiding away and pausing so that he would be prepared and strengthened to walk out his life purpose. He said after his encounter with God where he was radically transformed that he chose not to run straight to Jerusalem and jump right into public ministry. No, instead he ran to the Arabian Desert for three years. For Paul, passion wasn't the problem, but he knew that if he tried to move forward still carrying the baggage of his past it would keep him from embracing fully who he was becoming. We must understand that stepping into our calling always begins with a preparation phase.

We have to give God time—time to burn off our old mindsets and let go of the strategies that will hinder us from remaining where he wants to take us. Our past can haunt our present if we don't take the time to allow God's grace to wash away all that is hiding in the crevasses of our hearts. My 40-day journey revealed mindsets and strategies that had to go and, now, it was my turn to be obedient. Awareness and revelation always come with responsibility. There were new things that would be required of me if I wanted to *stay free*. Things I have had to lay before the Lord. Things I had to seek forgiveness for and do differently.

I had to intentionally choose to put my family first and carve out time for fun and play. I had to choose to stop striving and start resting in God's power at work in me and submitting to his way alone. I had to submit to God's timetable and stop hoarding manna like the Israelites as if God wasn't going to provide for me. I had to stop giving others a place and voice in my life that should be designated only for God. I had to ask my family to forgive me for making them feel second rate and I repented, asking God to forgive me for: trying to do his dream on my own as if it all depended on me, for seeking position over his presence, for being "scarcity scared", for failing to trust in his goodness, and for seeking applause and approval from man.

More freedom!

When God asked me to rest, it felt impossible at first and it terrified me a bit. I'll admit it, but what I realized was God wasn't setting me up for failure, he was setting me up for success. We simply can't survive where he wants to take us with our old mindsets and self-directed protective strategies leading the way. The protective strategies we created in the dark, won't work in the light! For me, I found peace and freedom by letting God's presence lead the way, setting aside my striving, getting my priorities in order, and finding my approval in God, not man. I no longer felt the pressure to perform and I experienced true joy for the first time in my life.

Encountering God's Heart for Yourself

I fear that many of you will be like me and take way too long to cease, to pause, to stop and experience the greatest gift ever known, God's rest. Hebrews 4:1 tells us that, "God's promise of entering his rest still stands, so we ought to tremble with fear that some of you might fail to experience it." My hope in creating, *The 40-Day Journey,* is that you will encounter God at a deeper level, discover your true identity, and experience the freedom to live out your life's purpose!

Will it be easy? Probably not. Your journey to freedom will require some things to die at the cross so that God can lead you to his path for you. Pastor of Elevation Church, Steven Furtick, says, "If you trust his promise you have to trust his path and it might lead to a cross." Are you willing to let some things die so that you can advance in your destiny? Give God the opportunity to take you on a detour for the next 40 days so that he can change the direction of your life forever!

In order to live out our callings, we have to be able to connect with God's heart and hear his voice. Developing a personal lifestyle of learning to gain God's perspective and apply it to our lives is the key to lasting freedom. God is always speaking. His love notes are everywhere. He is just hoping we will finally pause to notice.

The format for *The 40-Day Journey,* and learning to cease daily, was developed as I reflected on the process I use to hear God's heart. Obviously, God will speak to each individual person in his unique way, but I think there are a few principles that we can all follow. One is to come with an expectation that God wants to connect personally with you. Habakkuk had this expectation. He said, "I will climb to my watchtower and stand at my guardpost. There I will wait to see what the Lord says." God promptly replied to Habakkuk and asked him to write out the words he was about to speak (Habakkuk 2:1-2).

I too begin with an expectation that God will show up for me and I go to my post (my quiet place). I slow everything down and let the stillness in. If you are still running with your feet or your mind, you're going to struggle to hear God's heart. Worship music, time spent in prayer, and meditating on God's Word helps to prepare my heart and mind to get into a place of surrender. I often start with a simple prayer asking God to silence all other voices and allow me to hear his heart alone. Then I ask, "Lord, what do you want my heart to know today?" I take the time to examine my thoughts, and actions and give God the opportunity to bring to mind any places I need his perspective.

In true God-like fashion he always shows up and begins to speak to my heart. I write, without question, the words that form in my mind and try not to allow doubt to stop the flow. Once the words no longer come, that is when I stop, re-read, and evaluate what I have heard based on scripture and God's character. Keep in mind, God will never reveal to you things that go against his character or his Word. For example, we know from scripture that God is love and that he is always looking at us through a lens of love. So that means his words will never be shaming. You may feel convicted, but you should never feel condemned. He is gentle, yet, persuasive, especially, with the areas in our hearts that are hard to look at.

Know that God can use any avenue he chooses to speak directly to your heart. There is no one-way, right-way. Just be open. You may find that you hear him in the lyrics of a song, in the beauty of his creation, in the God-breathed words of scripture, or even through the kindness of another. Maybe it is just a whisper in your heart that cannot be denied. One thing is certain, he is speaking. We just have to pause to listen.

After receiving God's perspective, obedience must come next. We often struggle with this step because we doubt what we've heard. Obedience is the soil where trust can grow. We have to make a decision to believe and let our faith lead what we see. In the end, it all comes down to this. The degree of our obedience determines the level of our freedom. Obedience may require you to fight your old ways of thinking, to extend forgiveness that is due, to apologize to someone you've hurt, to break off an unhealthy relationship, or to surrender to God's way and lay at his feet your self-protective strategies. Let him take it. Place in his hands the things that are holding you back so that he can fill you with his peace that surpasses all understanding (Phil. 4:7).

A repentant heart is key. When we ask God for forgiveness for aligning our lives with lies and self-protective strategies instead of his truth, it breaks the power they hold over us. Set your intention on surrendering to God's will for you and aligning your actions with his truth. This process often happens in pieces, bit by bit and giving God what you can in the moment. He is patient with us. He knows that there are things we are going to struggle to let go of. Therefore, this process shouldn't be just another ritual but truly letting go as you are ready. It is a heart pursuit. If you are honestly seeking God's way, he will honor your efforts.

Then, finally, expect God's goodness and promises to be true for you! What he is revealing can be robbed by doubt. The enemy loves to gobble up like pack-man all the wonderful morsels that flow from God's heart to us. We must choose where we put our focus, so that we remain free (Galatians 5:1). If we aren't intentional about guarding our hearts and what we allow to have access within, it is easy to fall right back into our old ways of believing and being.

You may be questioning, "Can God really speak to me?" God's word makes it clear that he wants to speak to each one of us. When we ask God into our hearts, we automatically receive the Holy Spirit and it is the Spirit's job to reveal God's heart to us and guide us. First Corinthians 2:10 says that, "God revealed these things by his Spirit. For his Spirit searches out everything and shows us God's deep secrets." Ephesians 2:18 tells us that this gift is for everyone. "All of us can come to the Father through the same Holy Spirit because of what Christ has done for us." God makes it easy. We make it hard. He placed his very presence in our heart to partner with us and guide us. Seek. Knock. And his promise to you is that you will find him!

Sonya's 40-Day Journey—Lighting the Way

I was issued a challenge. Basically, I was to spend the next 40 days, for lack of better phrasing, being the opposite of myself. We all have our pasts: lies and experiences that cause our reactions and trigger our emotions in our current lives—good and bad. In my life, this past involves abandonment issues, distrust, insecurity, thick walls, a lot of emotional scar tissue, and unbeknownst to me, some unforgiveness. Okay, so truthfully, I guess I shouldn't have been surprised to find that one on the list, but it was wrapped up in pretty paper labeled "I'm totally good, I've got this."

Since my "normal" self would never want to share this journey with anyone, especially publicly, I decided to write about it. The challenge for me was to do the following three things:

1. Cease from self. Do not engage my protective strategies to keep my heart safe.
2. Trust in God's goodness and his desire to provide me with my every need.
3. Forgive. All the people.

Starting with number one. Not engaging in my protective strategies literally brought me to tears just thinking about it. We all have things we do at times to keep unsafe people from wounding us. Well, I may have a teensy issue with this happening in every—single—relationship in my life. There. I said it. I admitted the most awkward thing I can think of to you. That means if you know me personally, I may be very open with you, but you will never know the millions of wounds, thoughts, feelings or emotions running through me at any given moment. Even if I share, it's going to be very guarded. I am always waiting for you to quit me. Quit loving me, quit supporting me, quit wanting to hang out with me, quit being my friend, spouse, son, mother, father. It's actually a very lonely way to live. Ugh. That was certainly more truth than I expected to come out.

Oh, and on your way to quitting me, I'm waiting for you to hurt me. I will never have a confrontation with you because that would mean I may hurt you. Your feelings matter more than mine, so I will "eat my emotions" as my therapist says, in an effort to protect yours and prolong the relationship. Because if we squabble, you will certainly quit me. So during my 40 days, I'm was challenged to confront what terrified me and tear down the walls I have so carefully erected, allowing myself to be vulnerable.

Number two. Trust in God's goodness and his desire to provide me with my every need. WHAT?!?! Aren't we supposed to work for what we need? And how does one go about trusting when one has never been able to trust others? That is a foundational flaw in me that is quite difficult to wrap my head around. Yes, I know. I am a Christian. I love Jesus. But that doesn't make me perfect or mean I have everything in life all tidy on a shelf. I am pretty sure God knew I didn't trust him well before I typed the words on this page. I'm just being vulnerable (see #1).

Oh, number three—the old wolf in sheep's clothing. I would love to say this will be an easy one. My pride wants me to say I have no problems forgiving others. Often, that is entirely true. The unforgiveness I have is towards the people in my life that did not hold up their end of the relationship, causing most of the other items on that list way up above. There are some seriously deep wounds from some seriously important people. They are no longer part of my life so why am I allowing unforgiveness towards them to cause their wounds to continue seeping negativity into my life? Good question. Plus, the angry side of me asks myself why I would let them have any headspace or win by continuing to cause me pain.

Harboring unforgiveness will not only continue to cause me pain, it also effects my relationship with God. The Bible mentions forgiving over 140 times. I'd say it's a fairly important concept we are to practice. Even taking Jesus out of the equation, studies show it has physical, often serious, impacts on our bodies, such as heart conditions (hmmm ... ironic? I think not), high blood pressure, auto immune disorders and in one study of cancer patients, 60 percent had high levels of unforgiveness.

So, three full days into the challenge I struggled with all three things. I had "conversations" that needed to be held, people to forgive, and trust that needed to grow. I neglected to allow myself to be vulnerable by sharing my ideas during a meeting. I didn't voice my opinion on a project that was removed from my hands. I was left feeling like I was never going to pull off an entire 40 days. Since I was learning to do the opposite of what I had always done, rather than hide my feelings, I started sharing them. Instead of isolating myself and hiding away or behaving as if nothing was going on, I began to allow others to see the things that I would much rather have kept to myself.

So, that is why I'm sharing my story with you. I am being real. Here is a deeper look at my personally journey with R.E.S.T:

R- Relaxing my hold. I was learning to release the tight grip I had on my pain, my finances, my job, my life and the hardest one—those self-protective strategies.

E- Escaping my limiting mindset. I had to stop putting God in a box.

S- Start to depend on God. If I believe he is who he says he is, won't he do for me all that he says he will do?

T- Triumph! Be successful in forgiving, trusting God, and not depending on self-preservation during my 40 days.

Now that I have given you the general picture, let's look at the details. We'll start with unforgiveness. Apparently, I have been harboring some unforgiveness towards key people in my past. Due to choices they made, the child in me had some cracks in her foundation. Yes, they created those seriously deep wounds. Yes, I'm better without them in my life today. But are they really out of my life if unforgiveness is still holding a spot in my heart?

These issues are like an actual physical wound. If not treated properly, the unforgiveness forces the wounds to remain open, festering, becoming infected and filling my bloodstream with the negative results of unforgiveness. They were still causing me to feel broken because of the choices they inflicted on me as a child. I don't know about you but something about this makes me dig in my heels and think "oh heck no! You know longer get this kind of power in my life!" Funny thing about forgiveness. It's just like most of our emotions, a choice. I have to wake up each and every day and make a decision to forgive them for these transgressions. Until the day it finally sticks.

Trusting God. This is still a daily fight. Though, I am seeing him as I work through this obedience. I find myself enjoying my worship a little more, praying without even realizing I'm doing it, being amazed even more than I was before in his glorious artwork in nature. (I'm a sucker for a good sky!) I am still lacking trust in others, but I think I need to trust God more so

HE can show me what that should genuinely look like. Oh! And in order to not put God in a box, I'm praying big giant prayers that seem crazy, ridiculous and impossible. I want to see what awesome blessings he has set aside for me and the people I'm in prayer for. I'm praying for my future, for his will to be my will, for that path to be clear.

The Results

When I got to day 32, I realized I felt different! The difference is this: I finally found true joy. You'll never guess where... Nope. Well, maybe. Earlier that week when I met with my therapist, she said "maybe your forgiveness issue lies within yourself. Maybe it's not all about others."

Uhmmm...yuck. Who asked for that?

She sent me home to create a list of all the things I needed to forgive myself for. So, here it is:

- Conception. Yup. I had to forgive myself for being conceived. They weren't ready. They didn't want me. But I was so determined to burst forth, I didn't care. Selfish, I know. OH PLEASE! This was hardly my fault. But it's definitely on the list.
- Robbing my mother of her youth. Duh. This is because I insisted on being conceived.
- Being molested-twice. I should have protected my young self, better. I should have known that my friend's high school brother was not just going to play as a couple of third grade girls would. I should have instinctively known my grandfather was a serial child molester and karate chopped him every time he tried. Which leads to...
- Tearing apart the family. When I revealed said serial child molester to my parents.
- Being barren. This one I believe I am not alone in owing myself a little grace and forgiveness. If we can't conceive, it immediately becomes our fault. Forever. I literally told my husband once that he could leave me because I couldn't make babies. Luckily, he didn't hit me with the pain that flashed across his face. Probably earned it, but he didn't.
- Adopting my son. As much love, time, effort—as many prayers, hugs, kisses, snuggles, juice boxes, x-rays, turtles, geckos, fishing poles or hiking trails we piled on top of him, we were unable to undo what was done before us. This one hurts in a way I don't even know how to describe. So, I just don't. I don't ask. I don't inquire. I just ignore. But I need to forgive myself for not being able to save him from himself.
- And I need to forgive myself for it destroying my marriage.
- My x-husband. I need to forgive myself that I wasn't enough. Pretty enough. Perfect enough. Rich enough. Fun enough. Interesting enough. Skinny enough. Intelligent enough. Enough.
- My bio mom again. Ditto. Not enough.

- Getting fat. Yes, I was on medication for fertility treatments that ballooned me up rapidly. Had a hysterectomy so I was in menopause at 30. The perfect storm of fat storage in a woman. Starving allowed some loss. Exercise didn't. Medical treatments helped shed some but 55 pounds later, I'm still walking around like I'm wearing a small suit about to burst open.
- Getting thinner. Because it's just not enough yet, is it? Work harder. Eat less. Hide that chocolate. The point is, I felt shamed fat, I feel shamed less fat. That's what we are doing to ourselves.
- Not finishing college. Seems self-explanatory but it's really not. Do you want to know why? Oh, I have a million "reasons." But the truth is, I never felt worthy of success. I never deserved good, nice or happy. I settled into a career that pays the bills, I enjoy it, but I know is not my calling. Maybe I should forgive that too.

Well, I think that's the list. It's certainly a good start. The funny thing was, one morning after I finished my list, I was praying and heard the words, "Grace upon Grace." Okay. Whatever. But when my therapist asked me to write a list of my own personal unforgiveness issues, that became a flashing neon sign. Grace upon grace. Grace upon grace. Oh. Sure. Okay. Give myself grace upon grace. "For out of His fullness [the superabundance of His grace and truth] we have all received *grace upon grace* [spiritual blessing upon spiritual blessing, favor upon favor, and gift heaped upon gift]" (John 1:16, AMP). Grace means the **free** and **unmerited favor** of God.

Did you see what I bolded there for you? Grace is free. Unmerited. Favor. We get it just because we get it. We get it just because he gives it. We get it "just because" Jesus took that cross for us. If we don't have to earn it from God, the least we can do is put it to good use.

So, lovelies. I will be working on forgiveness towards myself. You should do the same. We don't deserve the grace, it's just there for us. So, grab it, let it free your heart and soul. Then spread it around like glitter! And find the true joy that is waiting around the corner.

Holly's 40-Day Journey—A Poetic Expression

In the earlier days of my walk with God, I would write short poems of simple words that the Lord was speaking. Since I tend to be impatient with my long-hand journaling, God gave me a way of recording my thoughts mixed with His words to me. As I started the 40-Day Journey, I began to reflect heavily in the "Pause, Sit and Soak In His Presence" sections. On certain days, the revelations were so tangible that I felt I would explode with hope and the goodness of God's love. There was something inside of me that wanted to burst out a song, a beautiful watercolor painting, or some other type of creativity.

Since I can't sing a lick and only own a Crayola watercolor paint set, I did the only thing an elementary school teacher could do—put her Dr. Seuss-type rhyming skills to work. I felt a flow in my heart that needed to pour out onto the pages. To my surprise, eighteen years after my last poem, simple words began to form my heart's message. As I realized what was happening, I just smiled and thanked God. It was immediately clear to me that this element of creativity was going to be a part of my healing process. What a sweet gift from the Father.

The following are a few of Holly's poetic revelations:

I'll Be Right Here
Day 12~By Holly Giles

Sitting here, my mind goes black

To make room for you, you're ushered back...

Into my thoughts, that run so deep
My own agendas, I no longer keep

They will melt away, with your sovereign hand

Drop images in, wherever they land.

Not my thoughts, but yours

Come on in, open the doors

Into my soul, piercing my heart

Stay close at all times, never drifting apart

I invite you, to the depths of my being

Clean up the mess, of the life you are seeing

Getting rid of soul ties, that bind me up tight

Letting go in Your name, cleansing in your sight.

My heart's desire is to be close to you
Experiencing supernaturally, what only you can do.

I long for your presence, to hear your word
Breathing it in, actively heard.

Only in your timing, you know best
You're molding me, and you know the rest.

I TRUST, yes I said it, and I'm willing to wait
As long as it takes, my God-designed fate.

To guide me with hope, on this journey so true
As you show me the path, my trust is in you.

Your gift to me is grace upon grace
I wow-fully accept, while I wait in this place.

I'll be right here.

I Choose You

Day 18~By Holly Giles

This has been a time of breakthrough

One for revelations, troubled times

And Fractured rhymes

That capture my heart for Him.

Contemplation and focus

One the One True Love.

His Presence.

Expectation.

Moments of Peace.

It's in the seeking

With the heart's light

Turns on bright

To identify the cracks.

Digging in deep

To a place of truth

And resting there—

Intentional.

Abiding.

Daily.

Heart surgery and

A renewal of the mind

The transforming kind

That Leaves you in a resting place.

A journey for the more

Where poems arise

And truth fills my soul

Like coffee fills my cup.

In pure satisfaction

Longing for more

He's opened the door

And welcomed me in.

To hear of His Word

Still active today

With great power and peace

And so... I pray.

Today and always

To seek more of you

Tapping into your strength...

Where freedom lives.

Put to test

Listening for your voice

I've been given a choice.

I choose YOU. A million times.

I choose you.

A Glimpse of Freedom

Day 28~By Holly Giles

You sent a friend

Who knows you well

To walk me through

And live to tell.

A story of redemption

Freedom has come

A lightness appears

A new beat to the drum.

Deep in the valley

Of a broken past

The sight of you appeared

A love so vast.

One that encompasses

And bids to overflow

There I saw Jesus

Standing aglow.

Waiting...

To be recognized

He was there all along

To reveal the truth

That I could be strong.

"Let me have it" he says

It's not yours to carry

Bask in His goodness

It doesn't have to be scary.

Claim the victory

That was meant long ago

My heart is mending

Move forward to grow.

Others who need me

Pass along my name,

Peace for my children

It's for all to claim.

A Few Guidelines for *The 40-Day Journey*:

1. Designate an accountability partner to walk alongside you and to be transparent with during this journey. We need each other. We were created for connection and it is in the place of deep intimacy with God and others that we heal.

2. Commit to spending time every day in *The 40-Day Journey* and completing as many sections as you can each day. The deeper you are willing to go, the more freedom you will experience!

3. Commit to being fully present and giving God your undivided attention during your devotional time. Find an undistracted space where you can pause to soak in all the treasures he wants to reveal to your heart and allow him the opportunity to breathe life into your soul.

4. Commit to a healthy eating plan during your 40-Day Journey. We are body, soul, and spirit. Which means the better we nourish our bodies the healthier our minds and emotions can be.

5. Commit to new ways of doing things. Don't just read the words that follow—*live them!* Step outside of your comfort zone and your regular limiting habits and do what you have never done, so that you can experience what you never thought you could!

6. Don't beat yourself up if you don't complete every item every day. Just promise yourself to not give up. Persevere through till the end no matter how long the journey takes you! It will all be worth it!

Encounter God

Day 1 Expectation and Praise

Thought of the day: Praise prepares your heart for what God is about to do!

I will CEASE today by choosing to:

Connect with God

Daily Word

Psalm 9:1 (TPT)

Lord, I will worship you with extended hands as my whole heart explodes with praise! I will tell everyone everywhere about your wonderful works and how your marvelous miracles exceed expectations!

Daily Worship

"Magnify" by We Are Messengers

Note here how this verse and song spoke directly to your heart:

_____

_____

_____

_____

_____

_____

_____

Examine My Heart

Lord, is there something in my heart that makes it hard for me to abandon myself fully to you in worship and believe that you will do great things in me and for me during this 40-day journey? What mountains do I need to begin to believe that you can move for me, Lord?

_____

_____

_____

_____

_____

_____

Allow God to Open My Heart to His View

I want you to know that I have plans for your good, plans to infuse hope and life into the dreams I have fashioned in your heart (Jeremiah, 29:11). The words I will speak into your heart during this journey will be hard for you to fathom at times, but know this, I see you and your situation so vastly different than what you can currently comprehend. It will require faith, but luckily, you only need faith the size of a tiny, little mustard seed and then I can move the mountains before you (Matthew, 17:20). Take this journey with me and watch me do immeasurably more than you could ever think, dream, or imagine in your life (Ephesians, 3:20). Walk to the edge of the sea before you, the sea you don't believe you can cross and take that first step. Feel the coolness of the water on your feet and watch as I begin to part the sea before you. I promise to make a way where there seems to be no way! I did it for Moses, and I can do it for you.

Surrender to God's Way

In this time of prayer visualize walking to the edge of the sea you thought you would never cross and taking that first step. God will meet you there. Be willing to hand over to him anything that you need to cease from that hinders your praise and ability to believe that God can do the impossible in your life during this 40-day journey. Break the power of any limiting mindsets (things you speak or believe) and protective strategies (things you do) that are holding you back by asking God to forgive you for partnering with views and actions that don't line up with his truth!

Write your own personal prayer of surrender here:

_____

_____

_____

_____

_____

_____

_____

_____

_____

_____

_____

_____

_____

_____

Expect God to Move on My Behalf

Expect mountains to move and the seas to be parted before you as you let go of the past and embrace what God has for you now. The waters before you are no match for God's presence inside you! Sing his praise. Thank him for what he is about to do in your life through the next 40 days and beyond!

Visualize a truth-filled thought based on what God revealed to your heart today and renew your mind in it all day long. Speak it, repeat it, be it!

My truth-focused thought for today:

_____

_____

Pause, Sit and Soak In His Presence

Sit and soak in the beauty of what God revealed to your heart today. Grant yourself the freedom to visualize fully and creatively express the thoughts, impressions, or images that come to your mind in any format that is best for you. Write, draw, paint, or collage allowing the images and words to flow freely from your heart so that your eyes can capture hope for the journey.

Mining Deeper

To mine is to dig deep and uncover treasures once hidden. It requires a search with the eyes and a heart that hungers for more. It is a willingness to explore unknown territory while trusting in the One leading the way. Over the course of the next few days, weeks, and months watch for how God continues to unfold deeper layers of truth regarding the area he spotlighted in your heart today. He rarely uncovers every layer all at once, because more than anything he wants daily intimacy with you. He wants you to mine the depths of his heart and as you do, he will uncover treasures before your eyes that will lead you to greater levels of freedom. Come back to this space to record and make note of the treasures he is leading your heart to discover!

Fill your thoughts with my words until they penetrate deep into your spirit. Then as you unwrap my words, they will impart true life and radiant health into the very core of your being.

Proverbs 4:21-22 (TPT)

Mining Topic: The place in my heart in need of God's view.

_____

My God-Directed Discoveries:

_____

_____

_____

_____

_____

_____

_____

_____

_____

_____

_____

_____

_____

_____

_____

_____

Day 2 Your View of God

Thought of the day: How you see God determines everything.

I will CEASE today by choosing to:

Connect with God

Daily Word

Ephesians 1:18 (NLT)

I pray that your hearts will be flooded with light so that you can understand the confident hope he has given to those he called.

Daily Worship

"Let There Be Light" by Hillsong Worship

Note here how this verse and song spoke directly to your heart:

_____

_____

_____

_____

_____

_____

_____

_____

Examine My Heart

How did your family of origin or life experiences shape your view of God? Do you trust God's intentions towards you or is there something from your past that makes it hard for you to trust him with all your heart? Ask God to open your eyes to his heart's intentions toward you.

_____

_____

_____

_____

_____

_____

Allow God to Open My Heart to His View

I can't wait to flood your heart with light so that you can finally see me as I am. This life brings pain and disappointment making you view me through a broken lens. I am not like anything you have ever known. I love completely and forgive easily. My heart is pure and flows with mercy toward you. My eyes delight at the sight of you. I don't want to point a finger at all that is wrong with you, I want to get close to you so that I can free your heart to see all that is right about you. You can stop hiding and striving. I've seen everything you have ever done and, yet, I accept you fully. My grace embraces all of who you are—including the things about yourself you want no one to see. Put your heart in my hands and let me fill it with light so that you no longer strive for my love but instead live your life full of my love. Letting me into every area of your heart during this journey is a pre-requisite for your freedom. If you let me in, I know my truth will set you free! (John, 8:32).

Surrender to God's Way

In this time of prayer allow your eyes to see God in a new light and open your heart to all he wants to be for you in this moment. Your heart is in the best of hands. Give God the space and time to expose any limiting mindsets (things you speak or believe) and protective strategies (things you do) that are hindering your ability to trust him with your heart during this 40-day journey. Break the power of any belief or strategy's hold over you by asking God to forgive you for partnering with views and actions that don't line up with his truth!

Write your own personal prayer of surrender here:

_____

_____

_____

_____

_____

_____

_____

_____

_____

_____

_____

_____

_____

_____

Expect God to Move on My Behalf

Thank God for his relentless pursuit of you. He wants to capture your heart—all of it!

Visualize a truth-filled thought based on what God revealed to your heart today and renew your mind in it all day long. Speak it, repeat it, be it!

My truth-focused thought for today:

Pause, Sit and Soak In His Presence

Sit and soak in the beauty of what God revealed to your heart today. Grant yourself the freedom to visualize fully and creatively express the thoughts, impressions, or images that come to your mind in any format that is best for you. Write, draw, paint, or collage allowing the images and words to flow freely from your heart so that your eyes can capture hope for the journey.

Mining Deeper

To mine is to dig deep and uncover treasures once hidden. It requires a search with the eyes and a heart that hungers for more. It is a willingness to explore unknown territory while trusting in the One leading the way. Over the course of the next few days, weeks, and months watch for how God continues to unfold deeper layers of truth regarding the area he spotlighted in your heart today. He rarely uncovers every layer all at once, because more than anything he wants daily intimacy with you. He wants you to mine the depths of his heart and as you do, he will uncover treasures before your eyes that will lead you to greater levels of freedom. Come back to this space to record and make note of the treasures he is leading your heart to discover!

Fill your thoughts with my words until they penetrate deep into your spirit. Then as you unwrap my words, they will impart true life and radiant health into the very core of your being.

Proverbs 4:21-22 (TPT)

Mining Topic: The place in my heart in need of God's view.

_____

My God-Directed Discoveries:

_____
_____
_____
_____
_____
_____
_____
_____
_____
_____
_____
_____
_____
_____
_____

Day 3 God's Relentless Love

Thought of the day: God is crazy about you!

I will CEASE today by choosing to:

Connect with God

Daily Word

Lamentation 3:22-23 (ESV)

The steadfast love of the Lord never ceases; his mercies never come to an end; they are new every morning; great is your faithfulness.

Daily Worship

"Reckless Love" by Cory Asbury of Bethel Music

Note here how this verse and song spoke directly to your heart:

_____

_____

_____

_____

_____

_____

_____

_____

Examine My Heart

What do I believe about God's love? Is there a part of me that believes I have to earn it or don't deserve it? Do I trust that God accepts me completely or do I believe there are some parts of me not even God could love?

_____

_____

_____

_____

_____

_____

Allow God to Open My Heart to His View

Walking on a curvy pebble path along a river bank you suddenly realize you're not alone as God slips his hand into yours. He pauses and gently lifts your chin asking you to look in his direction. His excitement can barely be contained in this moment alone with you. He has something life changing for you to experience. Your first inclination is to dart your gaze and resist, but like a toddler who just can't wait, he insists. A tear forms in his eye as he looks at you knowing you haven't even begun to grasp how crazy he is about you. He looks at you intently and says, "I love you completely. I've seen every crevice of your heart, everything you have ever done, and *nothing* can keep me from loving you!" Your heart and mind are in tug-a-war as you question, "How is this kind of love even possible? A love that has seen every part of me yet loves me completely!"

Surrender to God's Way

In this time of prayer let God's love pour into your heart in a way you never have before. Ask him to show you what his ceaseless love looks like. Let his mercies, that never end and are new every morning, flood into every area of your heart that is struggling to believe he loves you completely. Lay your head on his shoulder and soften into his embrace. Give God the space and time to expose any limiting mindsets (things you speak or believe) and protective strategies (things you do) that are hindering your ability to let God love you completely. Break the power of any belief or strategy's hold over you by asking God to forgive you for partnering with views and actions that don't line up with his truth!

Write your own personal prayer of surrender here:

_____

_____

_____

_____

_____

_____

_____

_____

_____

_____

_____

_____

Expect God to Move on My Behalf

Thank God for his love that never ceases and his mercies that are like a cleansing shower pouring over you *every* morning. A fresh slate is waiting for you!

Visualize a truth-filled thought based on what God revealed to your heart today and renew your mind in it all day long. Speak it, repeat it, be it!

My truth-focused thought for today:

_____

_____

Pause, Sit and Soak In His Presence

Sit and soak in the beauty of what God revealed to your heart today. Grant yourself the freedom to visualize fully and creatively express the thoughts, impressions, or images that come to your mind in any format that is best for you. Write, draw, paint, or collage allowing the images and words to flow freely from your heart so that your eyes can capture hope for the journey.

Mining Deeper

To mine is to dig deep and uncover treasures once hidden. It requires a search with the eyes and a heart that hungers for more. It is a willingness to explore unknown territory while trusting in the One leading the way. Over the course of the next few days, weeks, and months watch for how God continues to unfold deeper layers of truth regarding the area he spotlighted in your heart today. He rarely uncovers every layer all at once, because more than anything he wants daily intimacy with you. He wants you to mine the depths of his heart and as you do, he will uncover treasures before your eyes that will lead you to greater levels of freedom. Come back to this space to record and make note of the treasures he is leading your heart to discover!

Fill your thoughts with my words until they penetrate deep into your spirit. Then as you unwrap my words, they will impart true life and radiant health into the very core of your being.

Proverbs 4:21-22 (TPT)

Mining Topic: The place in my heart in need of God's view.

_____

My God-Directed Discoveries:

_____

_____

_____

_____

_____

_____

_____

_____

_____

_____

_____

_____

_____

_____

_____

_____

_____

Day 4 God's Character

Thought of the day: God is one hundred percent good, one hundred percent of the time!

I will CEASE today by choosing to:

Connect with God

Daily Word

Genesis 50:20 (MSG)

Don't you see, you planned evil against me, but God used those same plans for good.

Daily Worship

"Sing My Way Back" by Steffany Gretzinger

Note here how this verse and song spoke directly to your heart:

_____

_____

_____

_____

_____

_____

_____

_____

_____

_____

Examine My Heart

Is there a hidden hurt in your heart that makes you question God's goodness? Has your view of God been tainted by the unexpected twists and turns of life? Ask God to help you sing your way back to his heart once again and believe in who he wants to be for you. (i.e. loving, forgiving, kind, accepting, safe, dependable, trustworthy).

_____

_____

_____

_____

_____

Allow God to Open My Heart to His View

I want you to hear my heart for you today. I long for you to understand that I can be nothing but *good*. My heart hurts for you in the moments you feel disappointed and broken by this life. I've collected your every tear—longing to free you from the hurt they expressed. Place in my hands your heartache so that I can turn it around for good in your life. I'll wait patiently for you to trust me again. I know there have been times when your experiences have made you questioned my goodness. Just know that I want to comfort you, shower mercy on you, be near you, encourage you, rescue you, protect you, defend you, be generous to you, guide you, purify you, heal you, restore you, and love you with all that I am. Give me the opportunity to prove to you that I am trustworthy, compassionate, unchanging, faithful, forgiving, slow to anger, all-knowing, and limitless. I know how to be your heart-mender, your fear-taker, your savior, your dwelling place, your friend, your advocate, your victory, and your dream-igniter! Let me show you *who* I am in you.

Surrender to God's Way

In this time of prayer let God reveal his true character to you. Give God the space and time to expose any limiting mindsets (things you speak or believe) and protective strategies (things you do) that are hindering your ability to trust in God's goodness and faithfulness. Break the power of any belief or strategy's hold over you by asking God to forgive you for partnering with views and actions that don't line up with his truth!

Write your own personal prayer of surrender here:

_____

_____

_____

_____

_____

_____

_____

_____

_____

_____

_____

_____

_____

_____

Expect God to Move on My Behalf

Expect God's faithfulness to work all things for good in your life as you seek his heart. It is the safest, most peace-filled, gentle place you will ever encounter.

Visualize a truth-filled thought based on what God revealed to your heart today and renew your mind in it all day long. Speak it, repeat it, be it!

My truth-focused thought for today:

_____

_____

Pause, Sit and Soak In His Presence

Sit and soak in the beauty of what God revealed to your heart today. Grant yourself the freedom to visualize fully and creatively express the thoughts, impressions, or images that come to your mind in any format that is best for you. Write, draw, paint, or collage allowing the images and words to flow freely from your heart so that your eyes can capture hope for the journey.

Mining Deeper

To mine is to dig deep and uncover treasures once hidden. It requires a search with the eyes and a heart that hungers for more. It is a willingness to explore unknown territory while trusting in the One leading the way. Over the course of the next few days, weeks, and months watch for how God continues to unfold deeper layers of truth regarding the area he spotlighted in your heart today. He rarely uncovers every layer all at once, because more than anything he wants daily intimacy with you. He wants you to mine the depths of his heart and as you do, he will uncover treasures before your eyes that will lead you to greater levels of freedom. Come back to this space to record and make note of the treasures he is leading your heart to discover!

Fill your thoughts with my words until they penetrate deep into your spirit. Then as you unwrap my words, they will impart true life and radiant health into the very core of your being.

Proverbs 4:21-22 (TPT)

Mining Topic: The place in my heart in need of God's view.

_____

My God-Directed Discoveries:

_____
_____
_____
_____
_____
_____
_____
_____
_____
_____
_____
_____
_____
_____
_____

Day 5 God's Promises

Thought of the Day: God's promises are the most powerful words ever spoken!

I will CEASE today by choosing to:

Connect with God

Daily Word

Psalm 139:8 (TPT)

You keep every promise you've ever made to me! Since your love for me is constant and endless, I ask you, Lord, to finish every good thing that you've begun in me!

Daily Worship

"Your Promises" by Elevation

Note here how this verse and song spoke directly to your heart:

_____

_____

_____

_____

_____

_____

_____

_____

Examine My Heart

Has discouragement taken over your heart and made you doubt the promises God has spoken in his Word? It is so easy when *our timing* and *God's timing* don't match to toss out his promises and allow hopelessness to take root in us. Ask God to help you place your hope in his ability to finish every good thing he has started in you and do as he has promised in your life!

_____

_____

_____

_____

_____

_____

Allow God to Open My Heart to His View

I want you to know the promises I have made to you so that when the storms of life come you will have my Word to hold onto and see you through. I promise that my sacrifice on the Cross covers every shame-filled moment you are struggling to let go of! I promise to give you my unfailing, unconditional, unshakeable love. I promise to fully forgive everything you release to me and erase it from my memory. I promise to live inside your heart, to guide you, comfort you, and speak words of life that refresh your weary soul. I promise to protect you, fight for you, and give you the strength to overcome any obstacle you face. I promise to never condemn you but to fully accept you. I promise to give you peace that is unexplainable. I promise to give you a new heart, fashioned with my desires for you. I promise to give you hope and a future designed only for you. I promise to never leave you! I promise to hear your prayers and intercede for you in heaven. I promise that no weapon formed against you will prosper. I promise to light your path. I promise to give you a forever home. I promise to never quit on you. I promise to transform, purify, and refine you by making you into my image. I promise to be your shelter in the storm. I promise to supply all your needs. I promise to clothe you with my righteousness. I promise to be your burden bearer. I promise to carry you in the moments you can't go on. I promise to rescue you from the pit and deliver you from troubled waters. I promise to make all your enemies flee at the mention of my name. I promise to drive fear out of your heart with my love. I promise to mend your wounds. I promise to break every chain place on you by the pain of this life. I promise to heal you and set you FREE!

Surrender to God's Way

In this time of prayer picture God's promises sinking deep into your heart—bringing new life and hope into every place suffocated by doubt and wounded by disappointment. Make a list of your needs and wounded places and pair each one with a promise God has given you in his Word. Pray with an expectation that his promises will come to pass in each of the areas you bring before him. Don't give up hope! Give God the time to fulfill what he has promised in your life. Watch it be done. Allow God to expose any limiting mindsets (things you speak or believe) and protective strategies (things you do) that are hindering your ability to place your hope in God's promises. Break the power of any belief or strategy's hold over you by asking God to forgive you for partnering with views and actions that don't line up with his truth!

Write your own personal prayer of surrender here:

_____

_____

_____

_____

_____

Expect God to Move on My Behalf

Expect God's promises to manifest in your life. Thank him for his promises and determine in your heart to believe that what he speaks will come to pass!

Visualize a truth-filled thought based on what God revealed to your heart today and renew your mind in it all day long. Speak it, repeat it, be it!

My truth-focused thought for today:

_____

_____

Pause, Sit and Soak In His Presence

Sit and soak in the beauty of what God revealed to your heart today. Grant yourself the freedom to visualize fully and creatively express the thoughts, impressions, or images that come to your mind in any format that is best for you. Write, draw, paint, or collage allowing the images and words to flow freely from your heart so that your eyes can capture hope for the journey.

Mining Deeper

To mine is to dig deep and uncover treasures once hidden. It requires a search with the eyes and a heart that hungers for more. It is a willingness to explore unknown territory while trusting in the One leading the way. Over the course of the next few days, weeks, and months watch for how God continues to unfold deeper layers of truth regarding the area he spotlighted in your heart today. He rarely uncovers every layer all at once, because more than anything he wants daily intimacy with you. He wants you to mine the depths of his heart and as you do, he will uncover treasures before your eyes that will lead you to greater levels of freedom. Come back to this space to record and make note of the treasures he is leading your heart to discover!

Fill your thoughts with my words until they penetrate deep into your spirit. Then as you unwrap my words, they will impart true life and radiant health into the very core of your being.

Proverbs 4:21-22 (TPT)

Mining Topic: The place in my heart in need of God's view.

_____

My God-Directed Discoveries:

_____

_____

_____

_____

_____

_____

_____

_____

_____

_____

_____

_____

_____

_____

_____

Day 6 His Sacrifice—Our Freedom

Thought of the day: You are free!

I will CEASE today by choosing to:

Connect with God

Daily Word

Isaiah 53: 5b (NLT)

He was beaten so we could be whole. He was whipped so we could be healed.

Daily Worship

"I Can't Believe" by Elevation

Note here how this verse and song spoke directly to your heart:

_____

_____

_____

_____

_____

_____

_____

_____

Examine My Heart

Have you paused to soak in the beauty of his sacrifice, realizing the price he paid so that you could know him and be fully free? Ask God to reveal the places in your heart you have yet to believe are paid in full.

_____

_____

_____

_____

_____

_____

_____

Allow God to Open My Heart to His View

There is nothing that my Cross cannot redeem and make whole. I sacrificed my life so that I could live inside your heart and show you how to live free. I never came to condemn you—though the enemy has done a good job of convincing my people otherwise. I came to set you free from every mistake that haunts your heart so that nothing would hinder the relationship I long to have with you now and for eternity. You see I knew every sin you would ever commit before I went to the Cross for you. Nothing stopped me from securing your freedom. There was no other way. I became the perfect, spotless sacrifice so that you could experience healing, wholeness, and freedom in the midst of a sin-drenched world. Now it is time, my dear, to embrace the freedom you've been freely given. It all hinges on this. Do you believe my sacrifice was enough to ensure your freedom and make you whole?

Surrender to God's Way

In this time of prayer slow down to picture the sacrifice he paid. Notice his shoulders carrying every sin you ever committed to the Cross and marking each one paid in full. His Cross was the only solution for our complete freedom. Give God the space and time to expose any limiting mindsets (things you speak or believe) and protective strategies (things you do) that are hindering your ability to trust that you are free indeed. Break the power of any belief or strategy's hold over you by asking God to forgive you for partnering with views and actions that don't line up with his truth!

Write your own personal prayer of surrender here:

_____

_____

_____

_____

_____

_____

_____

_____

_____

_____

_____

_____

_____

_____

Expect God to Move on My Behalf

Praise God that Jesus' sacrifice covers everything! Nothing is beyond his grace. The power of the Cross has set you free and now lives in you!

Visualize a truth-filled thought based on what God revealed to your heart today and renew your mind in it all day long. Speak it, repeat it, be it!

My truth-focused thought for today:

_____

_____

Pause, Sit and Soak In His Presence

Sit and soak in the beauty of what God revealed to your heart today. Grant yourself the freedom to visualize fully and creatively express the thoughts, impressions, or images that come to your mind in any format that is best for you. Write, draw, paint, or collage allowing the images and words to flow freely from your heart so that your eyes can capture hope for the journey.

Mining Deeper

To mine is to dig deep and uncover treasures once hidden. It requires a search with the eyes and a heart that hungers for more. It is a willingness to explore unknown territory while trusting in the One leading the way. Over the course of the next few days, weeks, and months watch for how God continues to unfold deeper layers of truth regarding the area he spotlighted in your heart today. He rarely uncovers every layer all at once, because more than anything he wants daily intimacy with you. He wants you to mine the depths of his heart and as you do, he will uncover treasures before your eyes that will lead you to greater levels of freedom. Come back to this space to record and make note of the treasures he is leading your heart to discover!

Fill your thoughts with my words until they penetrate deep into your spirit. Then as you unwrap my words, they will impart true life and radiant health into the very core of your being.

Proverbs 4:21-22 (TPT)

Mining Topic: The place in my heart in need of God's view.

My God-Directed Discoveries:

Day 7 Hearing God's Heart

Thought of the day: God can't wait to speak to your heart.

I will CEASE today by choosing to:

Connect with God

Daily Word

Isaiah 52: 6 (NLT)

But I will reveal my name to my people, and they will come to know its power. Then at last they will recognize that I am the one who speaks to them.

Daily Worship

"The More I Seek You" by Kari Jobe

Note here how this verse and song spoke directly to your heart:

_____

_____

_____

_____

_____

_____

_____

_____

_____

Examine My Heart

Do you struggle to believe that God wants to speak to your heart or when he does, do you let doubt creep in and make you question what you've heard? Ask God to reveal any beliefs you hold that would cause you to doubt God's desire to speak into your heart exactly what you need to hear in this moment.

_____

_____

_____

_____

_____

_____

Allow God to Open My Heart to His View

Out in the middle of a flowing meadow, you see a ladder extending down from a cloud above. It draws you to it like a current you can't quite explain. You feebly climb up the ladder and peek your head above the clouds. You see God sitting there waving excitedly for you to come over. For a second you pause, sure he doesn't mean you—he must be waving to someone else. Looking behind your shoulder you see that no one else is there. You question, "Could God really be that excited to see me?" You finally decide to take his invitation and sit on the cloud with him. You dangle your feet together over the edge as God begins to ask you about your day. You laugh together. You cry together. Then God looks at you and says, "I am so glad you're here! I have waited patiently for the day you would share your heart with me. I want to be with you in the highs, the lows, and through the storms of your life. Let me walk beside you always so that when the unexpected comes, I can show you the way through."

Surrender to God's Way

In this time of prayer let God draw you into his presence far above the cares of this world so that he can give you his higher perspective. When you seek his truth, it will bubble up from within you. Ask God for the courage to overcome any doubt. Give him the space and time to expose any limiting mindsets (things you speak or believe) and protective strategies (things you do) that are hindering your ability to believe that God wants to speak directly to your heart. Break the power of any belief or strategy's hold over you by asking God to forgive you for partnering with views and actions that don't line up with his truth!

Write your own personal prayer of surrender here:

_____

_____

_____

_____

_____

_____

_____

_____

_____

_____

_____

Expect God to Move on My Behalf

Expect God to be excited to spend time with you and share his heart with you. His truth will reset your soul and free your mind to experience a whole new view.

Visualize a truth-filled thought based on what God revealed to your heart today and renew your mind in it all day long. Speak it, repeat it, be it!

My truth-focused thought for today:

_____

_____

Pause, Sit and Soak In His Presence

Sit and soak in the beauty of what God revealed to your heart today. Grant yourself the freedom to visualize fully and creatively express the thoughts, impressions, or images that come to your mind in any format that is best for you. Write, draw, paint, or collage allowing the images and words to flow freely from your heart so that your eyes can capture hope for the journey.

Mining Deeper

To mine is to dig deep and uncover treasures once hidden. It requires a search with the eyes and a heart that hungers for more. It is a willingness to explore unknown territory while trusting in the One leading the way. Over the course of the next few days, weeks, and months watch for how God continues to unfold deeper layers of truth regarding the area he spotlighted in your heart today. He rarely uncovers every layer all at once, because more than anything he wants daily intimacy with you. He wants you to mine the depths of his heart and as you do, he will uncover treasures before your eyes that will lead you to greater levels of freedom. Come back to this space to record and make note of the treasures he is leading your heart to discover!

Fill your thoughts with my words until they penetrate deep into your spirit. Then as you unwrap my words, they will impart true life and radiant health into the very core of your being.

Proverbs 4:21-22 (TPT)

Mining Topic: The place in my heart in need of God's view.

My God-Directed Discoveries:

Discover You

Day 8 Setting the Stage—Your Family of Origin

Thought of the day: Your past doesn't get to define where God wants to take you.

I will CEASE today by choosing to:

Connect with God

Daily Word

Galatians 4:5-7 (NLT)

God sent him to buy freedom for us who were slaves to the law, so that he could adopt us as his very own children. And because we are his children, God has sent the Spirit of his son into our hearts, prompting us to call out, Abba, Father. Now you are no longer a slave but God's own child, God has made you his heir.

Daily Worship

"No Longer Slaves" by Jonathan and Melissa Helser

"Abba" by Jonathan David Helser

Note here how this verse and song spoke directly to your heart:

_____

_____

_____

_____

_____

Examine My Heart

Our family of origin sets the stage for how we end up perceiving ourselves and the world around us. Take a moment to ponder how the scenes that played out in your life as a child, shaped your view of yourself, people, and the world. Ask God to reveal to you anything you experienced early in life that has made you question your true-identity in him and is hindering your ability now to accept the good gifts God has for you as his child. Obviously, we don't have the ability to choose the stage we grew up on, but we can open our hearts in this moment and allow God to set us free from replaying the past. We must begin to look honestly at the views our past experiences have created and question whether or not these views line up with the truth in God's Word.

_____

_____

_____

Allow God to Open My Heart to His View

My child, my hope is that you will understand how much I want to give you. Let me rearrange your view and how you have come to see your story so that I can open wide the doors to your future. I can't wait to show you all I have prepared for you. I want to overwhelm you with good things. I know your future. I have always known how your story was meant to unfold. Now I want you to see it too. Your past contains disappointments and hurts that are contaminating your ability to receive from me now as your loving father. I want to break all the chains from your past and from the generations before you. Let me love you as my very own. You are worthy of my care, affection, and heir to all I own. Everything I have is yours!

Surrender to God's Way

In this time of prayer let God reset the stage formed by your past experiences and allow him to completely rearrange your view. We all have family traits and patterns we want to be free from—things that nag us and frustrate us about ourselves—things that have been "passed down" and we believed this is "just the way it is". Ask God to break the hold these unhealthy patterns have had over your life and put an end to the repetition of the past in you and your future generations.

Give God the space and time to expose any limiting mindsets (things you speak or believe) and protective strategies (things you do) that were created from your past painful experiences and are now hindering your ability to see the stage God wants to set for your future. Break the power of any belief or strategy's hold over you by asking God to forgive you for partnering with views and actions that don't line up with his truth!

Write your own personal prayer of surrender here:

_____

_____

_____

_____

_____

_____

_____

_____

_____

_____

Expect God to Move on My Behalf

Expect God's perspective to completely rearrange how you see the hurtful scenes from your past. God has written an unbelievable ending to your story and he can't wait to provide everything you need for the future he has designed for you!

Visualize a truth-filled thought based on what God revealed to your heart today and renew your mind in it all day long. Speak it, repeat it, be it!

My truth-focused thought for today:

_____

_____

Pause, Sit and Soak In His Presence

Sit and soak in the beauty of what God revealed to your heart today. Grant yourself the freedom to visualize fully and creatively express the thoughts, impressions, or images that come to your mind in any format that is best for you. Write, draw, paint, or collage allowing the images and words to flow freely from your heart so that your eyes can capture hope for the journey.

Mining Deeper

To mine is to dig deep and uncover treasures once hidden. It requires a search with the eyes and a heart that hungers for more. It is a willingness to explore unknown territory while trusting in the One leading the way. Over the course of the next few days, weeks, and months watch for how God continues to unfold deeper layers of truth regarding the area he spotlighted in your heart today. He rarely uncovers every layer all at once, because more than anything he wants daily intimacy with you. He wants you to mine the depths of his heart and as you do, he will uncover treasures before your eyes that will lead you to greater levels of freedom. Come back to this space to record and make note of the treasures he is leading your heart to discover!

Fill your thoughts with my words until they penetrate deep into your spirit. Then as you unwrap my words, they will impart true life and radiant health into the very core of your being.

Proverbs 4:21-22 (TPT)

Mining Topic: The place in my heart in need of God's view.

My God-Directed Discoveries:

Day 9 The Ups and Downs—Timeline of Your Life

Thought of the day: There is no moment in your life beyond God's healing touch.

I will CEASE today by choosing to:

Connect with God

Daily Word

Romans 8:28 (TPT)

So we are convinced that every detail of our lives is continually woven together to fit into God's perfect plan of bringing good into our lives, for we are his lovers who have been called to fulfill his designed purpose.

Daily Worship

"Give Me Faith" by Elevation Worship

Note here how this verse and song spoke directly to your heart:

_____

_____

_____

_____

_____

_____

_____

_____

Examine My Heart

Draw a line in the middle of a paper and plot your life's course from birth to now. The things you write above the line are the moments you experienced the ups, the good, the blessings in your life and those things you write below are the moments when life pushed you down. These are the painful, skinned-knee moments you may be tempted to omit all together and not write down. The areas we want to avoid are the places within us most in need of healing and God's touch. They are the places we've tucked away, and never let anyone know about. What we don't reveal, cannot be healed! Being real with our hurts takes courage and leads the way to experiencing freedom.

When you look over your timeline, what have these ups and downs taught you to believe about yourself, God, people, and your future? What moments are holding you back from believing you're enough, God is there for you, people can be trusted, and that God has great and mighty plans for your life?

Allow God to Open My Heart to His View

I've seen your every hurt. I know this life sometimes makes no sense and causes you to doubt my presence, but I have always been there. I have never left your side. I know people made choices along your timeline that scarred you deeply and broke your heart. I want to mend all that now. I want to turn the situations that have stolen your song into places of your greatest strength! Then your light will shine forth like the noon-day sun! Let nothing stop your praise. Let it bellow from the depths of your soul and break you free. Hold nothing back. I want to hear the cries of your heart as you collapse into my arms. I am faithful to transform into good what you place within my hands. Give me all of your story so that we can write a beautiful future together.

Surrender to God's Way

In this time of prayer be real and vulnerable with God about your experiences, your disappointments, your hurts, and take time to praise him for the good in your life as well. Talk to him like a trusted friend and let nothing remain hidden. Give God the space and time to expose any limiting mindsets (things you speak or believe) and protective strategies (things you do) that are hindering your ability to believe that God wants to be there for you in all the ups and downs of your life and that you are worthy of God's healing touch no matter what your timeline contains. Break the power of any belief or strategy's hold over you by asking God to forgive you for partnering with views and actions that don't line up with his truth!

Write your own personal prayer of surrender here:

Expect God to Move on My Behalf

Expect God to faithfully transform the hurts that you give back to him into good and allow him the *time* necessary to do it. We cannot help but to be forever changed in his presence!

Visualize a truth-filled thought based on what God revealed to your heart today and renew your mind in it all day long. Speak it, repeat it, be it!

My truth-focused thought for today:

_____

_____

Pause, Sit and Soak In His Presence

Sit and soak in the beauty of what God revealed to your heart today. Grant yourself the freedom to visualize fully and creatively express the thoughts, impressions, or images that come to your mind in any format that is best for you. Write, draw, paint, or collage allowing the images and words to flow freely from your heart so that your eyes can capture hope for the journey.

Mining Deeper

To mine is to dig deep and uncover treasures once hidden. It requires a search with the eyes and a heart that hungers for more. It is a willingness to explore unknown territory while trusting in the One leading the way. Over the course of the next few days, weeks, and months watch for how God continues to unfold deeper layers of truth regarding the area he spotlighted in your heart today. He rarely uncovers every layer all at once, because more than anything he wants daily intimacy with you. He wants you to mine the depths of his heart and as you do, he will uncover treasures before your eyes that will lead you to greater levels of freedom. Come back to this space to record and make note of the treasures he is leading your heart to discover!

Fill your thoughts with my words until they penetrate deep into your spirit. Then as you unwrap my words, they will impart true life and radiant health into the very core of your being.

Proverbs 4:21-22 (TPT)

Mining Topic: The place in my heart in need of God's view.

My God-Directed Discoveries:

Day 10 Identifying Your Likes, Wants, and Desires

Thought of the day: Your likes, desires, and needs matter to God.

I will CEASE today by choosing to:

Connect with God

Daily Word

Psalm 37: 4 (AMP)

Delight yourself in the Lord, and he will give you the desires and petitions of your heart.

Daily Worship

"Let It Happen" by Andrea Marie of United Pursuit

Note here how this verse and song spoke directly to your heart:

_____

_____

_____

_____

_____

_____

_____

_____

Examine My Heart

What are the petitions of your heart? Do you honestly know yourself and your truest desires enough to ask for them if God said to you today, "Ask anything in my name, my dear, and I will give it to you" (Matthew 7:7)? Is it possible that you have neglected your needs for so long trying to please everyone else that you have lost yourself in the process? Deep down, have you come to believe that your needs are unimportant and not worthy of attention? If so, ask God to reveal when this belief began.

_____

_____

_____

_____

_____

Allow God to Open My Heart to His View

I made you full of life with your own unique likes, needs, and desires that deserve your attention. I want you to delight yourself in me and let me show you all the vibrant colors I placed within you that make you, you! Let me take you back to the beginning before life began to distort your vision of yourself and help you find "You" again. You may have wandered off the path for a brief time, but now you will find yourself again through my eyes. I created you for such a time as this. I want you to pause and just spend time discovering "You". I know this may feel awkward or uncomfortable, but I want you to learn to embrace how I intricately designed every part of you. You matter. Your needs, hopes, cares, and desires matter. Pour them out before me. My ears are wide open!

Surrender to God's Way

In this time of prayer let God help you rediscover "You" again. Give God the space and time to expose any limiting mindsets (things you speak or believe) and protective strategies (things you do) that are hindering your ability to believe that you matter and that your needs and the desires of your heart are important to him. Break the power of any belief or strategy's hold over you by asking God to forgive you for partnering with views and actions that don't line up with his truth!

Write your own personal prayer of surrender here:

_____

_____

_____

_____

_____

_____

_____

_____

_____

_____

_____

_____

_____

_____

_____

Expect God to Move on My Behalf

Expect God to care affectionately for you. He loves every part of you. He gets you. He knows you and he designed you with a purpose in mind. The better you get to know your true self, the greater the impact you will have on the world!

Visualize a truth-filled thought based on what God revealed to your heart today and renew your mind in it all day long. Speak it, repeat it, be it!

My truth-focused thought for today:

_____

_____

Pause, Sit and Soak In His Presence

Sit and soak in the beauty of what God revealed to your heart today. Grant yourself the freedom to visualize fully and creatively express the thoughts, impressions, or images that come to your mind in any format that is best for you. Write, draw, paint, or collage allowing the images and words to flow freely from your heart so that your eyes can capture hope for the journey.

Mining Deeper

To mine is to dig deep and uncover treasures once hidden. It requires a search with the eyes and a heart that hungers for more. It is a willingness to explore unknown territory while trusting in the One leading the way. Over the course of the next few days, weeks, and months watch for how God continues to unfold deeper layers of truth regarding the area he spotlighted in your heart today. He rarely uncovers every layer all at once, because more than anything he wants daily intimacy with you. He wants you to mine the depths of his heart and as you do, he will uncover treasures before your eyes that will lead you to greater levels of freedom. Come back to this space to record and make note of the treasures he is leading your heart to discover!

Fill your thoughts with my words until they penetrate deep into your spirit. Then as you unwrap my words, they will impart true life and radiant health into the very core of your being.

Proverbs 4:21-22 (TPT)

Mining Topic: The place in my heart in need of God's view.

_____

My God-Directed Discoveries:

_____

_____

_____

_____

_____

_____

_____

_____

_____

_____

_____

_____

_____

_____

_____

_____

Day 11 Your Unique Personality Style

Thought of the day: God perfectly design you with the exact ingredients he wanted you to possess and purposely left out the ones he didn't.

I will CEASE today by choosing to:

Connect with God

Daily Word

Psalms 139:13-15 (TPT)

You formed my innermost being, shaping my delicate inside and my intricate outside, and wove them all together in mother's womb. I thank you, God, for making me so mysteriously complex! Everything you do is marvelously breathtaking. It simply amazes me to think about it! How thoroughly you know me, Lord! You even formed every bone in my body when you created me in the secret place, carefully, skillfully shaping me from nothing to something.

Daily Worship

"Masterpiece" by Danny Gokey

Note here how this verse and song spoke directly to your heart:

_____

_____

_____

_____

_____

_____

Examine My Heart

God didn't make a mistake by giving you the personality he did. Do you sometimes doubt that God knew exactly what he was doing when he created you? Can you begin to allow God to use your every weakness to prove that his strength is within you?

_____

_____

_____

_____

As a bonus activity, you could choose to pause here and take a personality inventory. The Enneagram or the 16 Personalities online test can help you take a deeper look at your unique personality style. You can find them here: (Please note I cannot verify the security of these sites. The sites listed are free options I have personally taken, but please use your own discretion.)

- https://enneagramtypetest.com/

(Once you find out what number you are, be sure to view an amazing series from Sandals Church on the Enneagram and your specific personality on YouTube!)

- https://www.16personalities.com/free-personality-test

Allow God to Open My Heart to His View

I designed you with every inch of you in mind. I gave you the characteristics I wanted you to possess and now I am asking you to trust me with the rest. You see life requires that you partner with me to be complete. I am the other half of you. Any weakness you feel within, is mine to complete. Let me continue to transform you and use the personality I gave you to do what only we can do together. I formed you with my very hands and breathed life into your soul. I whispered into your ear as I formed you in the womb letting you know you are mine! I handpicked every ingredient that makes you, you. I am so pleased with what I created. My heart smiles with delight every time I look at you!

Surrender to God's Way

In this time of prayer picture God taking his time and thoughtfully placing all the ingredients within you that make you unique. See him breath his life into your heart and imagine him completing any place you feel is lacking within you with his presence. Thank him that he thoughtfully planned your specific design. Give God the space and time to expose any limiting mindsets (things you speak or believe) and protective strategies (things you do) that are hindering your ability to believe that God designed you perfectly and made no mistake. Break the power of any belief or strategy's hold over you by asking God to forgive you for partnering with views and actions that don't line up with his truth!

Write your own personal prayer of surrender here:

_____

_____

_____

_____

_____

_____

_____

Expect God to Move on My Behalf

Expect God's presence within you to transform any area of weakness into strength! Thank him for making you with the exact ingredients that perfectly fit together to create you.

Visualize a truth-filled thought based on what God revealed to your heart today and renew your mind in it all day long. Speak it, repeat it, be it!

My truth-focused thought for today:

Pause, Sit and Soak In His Presence

Sit and soak in the beauty of what God revealed to your heart today. Grant yourself the freedom to visualize fully and creatively express the thoughts, impressions, or images that come to your mind in any format that is best for you. Write, draw, paint, or collage allowing the images and words to flow freely from your heart so that your eyes can capture hope for the journey.

Mining Deeper

To mine is to dig deep and uncover treasures once hidden. It requires a search with the eyes and a heart that hungers for more. It is a willingness to explore unknown territory while trusting in the One leading the way. Over the course of the next few days, weeks, and months watch for how God continues to unfold deeper layers of truth regarding the area he spotlighted in your heart today. He rarely uncovers every layer all at once, because more than anything he wants daily intimacy with you. He wants you to mine the depths of his heart and as you do, he will uncover treasures before your eyes that will lead you to greater levels of freedom. Come back to this space to record and make note of the treasures he is leading your heart to discover!

Fill your thoughts with my words until they penetrate deep into your spirit. Then as you unwrap my words, they will impart true life and radiant health into the very core of your being.

Proverbs 4:21-22 (TPT)

Mining Topic: The place in my heart in need of God's view.

My God-Directed Discoveries:

Day 12 Daily Habits and Self-Care Routines

Thought of the day: For my body, soul, and spirit to be healthy, I must choose to nourish, protect, and cherish myself.

I will CEASE today by choosing to:

Connect with God

Daily Word

Ephesians 5:29-30 (AMP)

For no one ever hated his own body, but [instead] he nourishes and protects and cherishes it, just as Christ does the church, because we are members [parts] of his body.

Daily Worship

"Alive In You" by Jesus Culture

Note here how this verse and song spoke directly to your heart:

_____

_____

_____

_____

_____

_____

_____

Examine My Heart

How healthy are your habits? Are you being diligent about taking care of your physical needs as well as your spiritual and emotional needs? Ask God to reveal to your heart areas that need improvement so that you can become the best version of yourself. How well you take care of your body, soul, and spirit is the foundation for your physical health, emotional stability, and your spiritual usability in Christ. Take time to discover your unique self-care needs and evaluate your habits. Look honestly at whether you are doing things that fill you up or drain you of the vital nutrients your body, soul, and spirit need to thrive.

_____

_____

_____

Allow God to Open My Heart to His View

Choose habits that nourish you and bring life to your soul. Taking care of your physical, emotional, and spiritual needs will give you the stamina and stability required to overcome and thrive in this life. I gave your body the ability to heal itself, but I need you to fill it with the right nutrients. I made your mind so than you could choose what you focus on. Stabilize your emotions by focusing on my truth. I made your spirit to crave vital time with me because there are simply places only I can fill. For balance and wholeness to be possible, you must address your body, soul, and spirit needs.

Surrender to God's Way

In this time of prayer be honest with yourself and let God reveal to your heart the habits you've chosen that are not allowing your physical, emotional, or spiritual needs to be met. Give God the space and time to expose any limiting mindsets (things you speak or believe) and protective strategies (things you do) that are hindering your ability to address your needs and replenish your body, soul, and spirit. Break the power of any belief or strategy's hold over you by asking God to forgive you for partnering with views and actions that don't line up with his truth!

Write your own personal prayer of surrender here:

_____

_____

_____

_____

_____

_____

_____

_____

_____

_____

_____

_____

_____

_____

_____

Expect God to Move on My Behalf

Expect God to help you form healing, healthy habits that give you the strength and stability to live the abundant life he wants to give you. When you do your part to nourish, cherish, and protect your body, soul, and spirit, God can do his.

Visualize a truth-filled thought based on what God revealed to your heart today and renew your mind in it all day long. Speak it, repeat it, be it!

My truth-focused thought for today:

_____

_____

Pause, Sit and Soak In His Presence

Sit and soak in the beauty of what God revealed to your heart today. Grant yourself the freedom to visualize fully and creatively express the thoughts, impressions, or images that come to your mind in any format that is best for you. Write, draw, paint, or collage allowing the images and words to flow freely from your heart so that your eyes can capture hope for the journey.

Mining Deeper

To mine is to dig deep and uncover treasures once hidden. It requires a search with the eyes and a heart that hungers for more. It is a willingness to explore unknown territory while trusting in the One leading the way. Over the course of the next few days, weeks, and months watch for how God continues to unfold deeper layers of truth regarding the area he spotlighted in your heart today. He rarely uncovers every layer all at once, because more than anything he wants daily intimacy with you. He wants you to mine the depths of his heart and as you do, he will uncover treasures before your eyes that will lead you to greater levels of freedom. Come back to this space to record and make note of the treasures he is leading your heart to discover!

Fill your thoughts with my words until they penetrate deep into your spirit. Then as you unwrap my words, they will impart true life and radiant health into the very core of your being.

Proverbs 4:21-22 (TPT)

Mining Topic: The place in my heart in need of God's view.

My God-Directed Discoveries:

Day 13 What Makes Your Heart Light Up?

Thought of the day: God fashioned a unique light within your heart that cannot wait to be set free.

I will CEASE today by choosing to:

Connect with God

Daily Word

Psalms 139:1 (NLT)

O Lord, you have examined my heart and know everything about me.

Daily Worship

"Set a Fire" by Will Reagan & United Pursuit

Note here how this verse and song spoke directly to your heart:

_____

_____

_____

_____

_____

_____

_____

Examine My Heart

Ask God to reveal to you any place inside that is holding you back from allowing your heart to dream and believe that he has big plans for your life? What is the one thing you would do if fear didn't stop you? In what areas of your life do you shine most and feel confident in your ability? What passion has been growing inside you? Have you been too afraid to listen?

_____

_____

_____

As a bonus activity, you could choose to investigate your strengths further by taking a spiritual gifts assessment or going to www.valuescentre.com and take the Personal Values Assessment under the "Mapping Values" tab to discover what drives and motivates you.

Allow God to Open My Heart to His View

I know your heart. I fashioned it and formed it by my very hands. I placed within you a light that is all your own—meant to shine in its own way. I understand your hesitation. I know that my dreams for you can feel overwhelming because they are bigger than your eyes can fully soak in. I do that on purpose so that your faith in me can grow. Learn to trust me with the details. I will finish what I began in you. From the moment you were conceived I breathed my plan into your heart and it began to pump through your veins. It is a part of you. Don't deny the passions, the fire, that I have ignited in you any longer. Let me whisper my truth into your ear daily so that you will be infused with the courage to fight for the vision I have given you. No eye has seen, or mind can conceive what I have planned for those who walk in my love and stare fear in the face and say, "Not my will, Lord, but yours be done!"

Surrender to God's Way

In this time of prayer ask God to reveal to you the light that he purposely fashioned for only your heart to hold. Imagine him placing it within you and a fire that cannot be contained growing inside. Give God the space and time to expose any limiting mindsets (things you speak or believe) and protective strategies (things you do) that are hindering your ability to believe that the light God fashioned in your heart is worthy to be shared with the world. Break the power of any belief or strategy's hold over you by asking God to forgive you for partnering with views and actions that don't line up with his truth!

Write your own personal prayer of surrender here:

_____

_____

_____

_____

_____

_____

_____

_____

_____

_____

_____

_____

_____

_____

Expect God to Move on My Behalf

Believe that God fashioned a light within your heart meant only for you. Expect him to finish what he began in you and let him lead the way.

Visualize a truth-filled thought based on what God revealed to your heart today and renew your mind in it all day long. Speak it, repeat it, be it!

My truth-focused thought for today:

_____

_____

Pause, Sit and Soak In His Presence

Sit and soak in the beauty of what God revealed to your heart today. Grant yourself the freedom to visualize fully and creatively express the thoughts, impressions, or images that come to your mind in any format that is best for you. Write, draw, paint, or collage allowing the images and words to flow freely from your heart so that your eyes can capture hope for the journey.

Mining Deeper

To mine is to dig deep and uncover treasures once hidden. It requires a search with the eyes and a heart that hungers for more. It is a willingness to explore unknown territory while trusting in the One leading the way. Over the course of the next few days, weeks, and months watch for how God continues to unfold deeper layers of truth regarding the area he spotlighted in your heart today. He rarely uncovers every layer all at once, because more than anything he wants daily intimacy with you. He wants you to mine the depths of his heart and as you do, he will uncover treasures before your eyes that will lead you to greater levels of freedom. Come back to this space to record and make note of the treasures he is leading your heart to discover!

Fill your thoughts with my words until they penetrate deep into your spirit. Then as you unwrap my words, they will impart true life and radiant health into the very core of your being.

Proverbs 4:21-22 (TPT)

Mining Topic: The place in my heart in need of God's view.

My God-Directed Discoveries:

Day 14 Your Greatest Fears

Thought of the day: Fear only has the power we give it.

I will CEASE today by choosing to:

Connect with God

Daily Word

2 Timothy 1:7 (TPT)

For God will never give you the spirit of fear, but the Holy Spirit who gives you mighty power, love, and self-control.

Daily Worship

"Here in Your Presence" by Elevation Worship

Note here how this verse and song spoke directly to your heart:

_____

_____

_____

_____

_____

_____

_____

_____

Examine My Heart

What are your greatest fears? What paralyzes you? Is it people's opinions? Is it the fear of failure? Is it the shame of your past? Ask God to reveal to you the fears he wants to free you from.

_____

_____

_____

_____

_____

_____

_____

_____

Allow God to Open My Heart to His View

Fear is not from me. I have given you a heart of love and power and ability to move mountains! Cast out every fear, every worry, every doubt and let me show you what we can accomplish together. The chains of your past were broken by my Cross, but now, you must slip your hands and feet out of the cuffs. Haven't you carried them long enough? When you have released what you were never meant to carry, you will suddenly feel an unexplainable lightness about you. I will never put weight on you, only take it from you. Shame is not from me, fear is not a part of you. It is just something you let in, but you can choose to release it. My mercy and love are falling upon you now. Let my love wash over you and pour into your heart so that I can drive out every fear it contains!

Surrender to God's Way

In this time of prayer picture God's love pouring over you and flooding your heart leaving no room for fear to remain. Visualize the Cross breaking every chain fear has put on you. Give God the space and time to expose any limiting mindsets (things you speak or believe) and protective strategies (things you do) that are hindering your ability to overcome your fears. Break the power of any belief or strategy's hold over you by asking God to forgive you for partnering with views and actions that don't line up with his truth!

Write your own personal prayer of surrender here:

_____

_____

_____

_____

_____

_____

_____

_____

_____

_____

_____

_____

_____

Expect God to Move on My Behalf

Expect God's love to drive out every fear in your heart! What you feed, will grow within you. Feed on God's love, and your fears will starve.

Visualize a truth-filled thought based on what God revealed to your heart today and renew your mind in it all day long. Speak it, repeat it, be it!

My truth-focused thought for today:

Pause, Sit and Soak In His Presence

Sit and soak in the beauty of what God revealed to your heart today. Grant yourself the freedom to visualize fully and creatively express the thoughts, impressions, or images that come to your mind in any format that is best for you. Write, draw, paint, or collage allowing the images and words to flow freely from your heart so that your eyes can capture hope for the journey.

Mining Deeper

To mine is to dig deep and uncover treasures once hidden. It requires a search with the eyes and a heart that hungers for more. It is a willingness to explore unknown territory while trusting in the One leading the way. Over the course of the next few days, weeks, and months watch for how God continues to unfold deeper layers of truth regarding the area he spotlighted in your heart today. He rarely uncovers every layer all at once, because more than anything he wants daily intimacy with you. He wants you to mine the depths of his heart and as you do, he will uncover treasures before your eyes that will lead you to greater levels of freedom. Come back to this space to record and make note of the treasures he is leading your heart to discover!

Fill your thoughts with my words until they penetrate deep into your spirit. Then as you unwrap my words, they will impart true life and radiant health into the very core of your being.

Proverbs 4:21-22 (TPT)

Mining Topic: The place in my heart in need of God's view.

_____

My God-Directed Discoveries:

_____

_____

_____

_____

_____

_____

_____

_____

_____

_____

_____

_____

_____

_____

_____

_____

Day 15 How Receptive Are You?

Thought of the day: When we let God's love in, he changes us from the inside out!

I will CEASE today by choosing to:

Connect with God

Daily Word

Zephaniah 3:17 (NLT)

For the Lord your God is living among you. He is a mighty savior. He will take delight in you with gladness. With his love, he will calm all your fears. He will rejoice over you with joyful songs.

Daily Worship

"One Thing Remains" by Kristian Stanfill

Note here how this verse and song spoke directly to your heart:

_____

_____

_____

_____

_____

_____

_____

_____

Examine My Heart

Do you find yourself resisting love, compliments, or gifts others want to give you? Deep within, do you feel undeserving of it all? Was there a moment your heart was wounded, and you decided to close it off for good? Ask God to reveal to you the moment shame entered your heart and built a wall that hinders you now from receiving love.

_____

_____

_____

_____

_____

Allow God to Open My Heart to His View

I saw the moment your heart broke and you decided to restrict love's admittance. Love may never have felt safe, and I know it scares you to open your heart again. Let my love calm all your fears in this moment. I want you to experience me dancing over you with delight and singing my love song in your ear. My heart longs for you to be swept away by my love for you. You deserve to be loved fully and completely. Let me say that again, YOU DESERVE TO BE LOVED FULLY AND COMPLETELY! I know at times you question whether your worthy, but I promise you, the voice of your shame has been lying to you all along. I want to rescue you from the chains of shame. Break free and run into my arms. My love for you never ends, never fails, never quits, never judges, and never turns away. Give me all of your heart, you already have all of mine!

Surrender to God's Way

In this time of prayer, picture yourself taking a sledgehammer to the walls shame has built around your heart. Brick by brick watch them fall. Then see God begin to dance and sing over you with delight. Suddenly your heart beats with a new vigor as his love surges through your veins and you know you've have been changed from the inside out!

Give God the space and time to expose any limiting mindsets (things you speak or believe) and protective strategies (things you do) that are hindering your ability to receive love. Break the power of any belief or strategy's hold over you by asking God to forgive you for partnering with views and actions that don't line up with his truth!

Write your own personal prayer of surrender here:

_____

_____

_____

_____

_____

_____

_____

_____

_____

_____

_____

_____

Expect God to Move on My Behalf

Expect God to dance over you with delight. For shame has no place in a heart so dearly loved!

Visualize a truth-filled thought based on what God revealed to your heart today and renew your mind in it all day long. Speak it, repeat it, be it!

My truth-focused thought for today:

Pause, Sit and Soak In His Presence

Sit and soak in the beauty of what God revealed to your heart today. Grant yourself the freedom to visualize fully and creatively express the thoughts, impressions, or images that come to your mind in any format that is best for you. Write, draw, paint, or collage allowing the images and words to flow freely from your heart so that your eyes can capture hope for the journey.

Mining Deeper

To mine is to dig deep and uncover treasures once hidden. It requires a search with the eyes and a heart that hungers for more. It is a willingness to explore unknown territory while trusting in the One leading the way. Over the course of the next few days, weeks, and months watch for how God continues to unfold deeper layers of truth regarding the area he spotlighted in your heart today. He rarely uncovers every layer all at once, because more than anything he wants daily intimacy with you. He wants you to mine the depths of his heart and as you do, he will uncover treasures before your eyes that will lead you to greater levels of freedom. Come back to this space to record and make note of the treasures he is leading your heart to discover!

Fill your thoughts with my words until they penetrate deep into your spirit. Then as you unwrap my words, they will impart true life and radiant health into the very core of your being.

Proverbs 4:21-22 (TPT)

Mining Topic: The place in my heart in need of God's view.

My God-Directed Discoveries:

Day 16 The Power of Connection

Thought of the day: Healthy relationships heal the soul.

I will CEASE today by choosing to:

Connect with God

Daily Word

Ecclesiastes 4:9 (NLT)

Two are better than one, for they can help each other succeed.

Daily Worship

"I Need You More" by Kim Walker

Note here how this verse and song spoke directly to your heart:

_____

_____

_____

_____

_____

_____

_____

Examine My Heart

On this journey to experiencing freedom, our connections (our relationships) are the single greatest factor that contributes to our success! No wonder, the enemy is hard at work seeking to destroy our relationships. How much do you let others know you? Are you a mask wearer? A performer? A people pleaser? Are you able to be completely real and vulnerable with anyone in your life? Do you feel free to express your struggles to God or do you try and perform for him too? How well do you connect with yourself? The less you know who you are, the more you will let others define you. Ask God to reveal to you any areas where you struggle to connect with him, yourself, or others.

_____

_____

_____

_____

_____

Allow God to Open My Heart to His View

I designed you with connection in mind. You thrive most when connected to me and others. The more you hide the less you connect. Authenticity and vulnerability give you back your power. When you choose to stop performing as an actor in the "picture-perfect life" your mask will no longer control you. You get to choose how you show up in this world. I guarantee you, the more open you are with your struggles, the more you will discover you're not alone! Being real, genuine, and unhindered by the opinions of others are keys that unlock the door to your freedom. Choose healthy, life-giving relationships that feed your dreams, pick you up when you fall down, and encourage your true self to shine through! Don't let the enemy defeat you by letting him isolate you. You were never meant to walk alone!

Surrender to God's Way

In this time of prayer ask God for the courage to be true to yourself and throw off the masks you've been hiding behind. Give God the space and time to expose any limiting mindsets (things you speak or believe) and protective strategies (things you do) that are hindering your ability to connect with God and others and cause you to hide who you really are. Break the power of any belief or strategy's hold over you by asking God to forgive you for partnering with views and actions that don't line up with his truth!

Write your own personal prayer of surrender here:

_____

_____

_____

_____

_____

_____

_____

_____

_____

_____

_____

_____

_____

Expect God to Move on My Behalf

Expect God to provide you with the courage and strength to tear off your masks! Your best chance for true connection, is when you allow the real you to emerge!

Visualize a truth-filled thought based on what God revealed to your heart today and renew your mind in it all day long. Speak it, repeat it, be it!

My truth-focused thought for today:

_____

_____

Pause, Sit and Soak In His Presence

Sit and soak in the beauty of what God revealed to your heart today. Grant yourself the freedom to visualize fully and creatively express the thoughts, impressions, or images that come to your mind in any format that is best for you. Write, draw, paint, or collage allowing the images and words to flow freely from your heart so that your eyes can capture hope for the journey.

Mining Deeper

To mine is to dig deep and uncover treasures once hidden. It requires a search with the eyes and a heart that hungers for more. It is a willingness to explore unknown territory while trusting in the One leading the way. Over the course of the next few days, weeks, and months watch for how God continues to unfold deeper layers of truth regarding the area he spotlighted in your heart today. He rarely uncovers every layer all at once, because more than anything he wants daily intimacy with you. He wants you to mine the depths of his heart and as you do, he will uncover treasures before your eyes that will lead you to greater levels of freedom. Come back to this space to record and make note of the treasures he is leading your heart to discover!

Fill your thoughts with my words until they penetrate deep into your spirit. Then as you unwrap my words, they will impart true life and radiant health into the very core of your being.

Proverbs 4:21-22 (TPT)

Mining Topic: The place in my heart in need of God's view.

_____

My God-Directed Discoveries:

_____
_____
_____
_____
_____
_____
_____
_____
_____
_____
_____
_____
_____
_____
_____
_____

Day 17 Your Emotions

Thought of the day: Emotions are the post-it notes of the soul, calling to us for daily recognition.

I will CEASE today by choosing to:

Connect with God

Daily Word

Psalm 18:6 (TPT)

I cried out to you in my distress, the delivering God, and from your temple-throne you heard my troubled cry. My sobs came right into your heart and you turned your face to rescue me.

(The Message Version)

My cry brings me right into his presence—a private audience!

Daily Worship

"It Is Well" by Kristene DiMarco & Bethel Music

Note here how this verse and song spoke directly to your heart:

_____

_____

_____

_____

_____

_____

_____

_____

Examine My Heart

How well do you know your inner world? If you took a snapshot of your heart what emotions does it currently display? What is the emotional climate of your life? Where do you tend to camp out? What are your beliefs about emotions? Do you embrace them or is your tactic just to ignore them all together?

Take a moment to ponder this:

"Neuroscience research shows that the only way we can change the way we feel is by becoming aware of our inner experience and learning to befriend what is going on inside ourselves" (Bessel Van Der Kolk, M.D., the founder and medical director for the Trauma Center in Massachusetts).

Our *only* chance of managing our emotions is to become aware of them! Avoidance just won't work because you cannot manage what you don't know exists. Emotions color our world. They describe our experience and are meant to propel action that connects us deeper with God, ourselves, others, and our purpose!

I challenge you to become a student of your emotions. Pause each day to note what your emotional climate is. You'll notice that the weather changes but that your preferred climate dictates its course. Journal, draw, write song lyrics, create your emotions in clay—do whatever you uniquely need to do to begin to get in touch with your inner experience and start addressing what your emotions are trying to spotlight for you.

_____

_____

_____

_____

_____

_____

_____

Allow God to Open My Heart to His View

I made you full of life and emotions so that you could experience love, joy, hope, peace, grace, compassion, and connect deeply with me and those around you. I know that emotions don't always feel good or seem controllable but those are the times I want you to cry out to me. I promise to meet you right where you are. I want to rescue you, direct you, comfort you, and lead you out of the storms that will come. Don't hide when you need me most. I already know the condition of your heart. I long to hold you close even in your despair, hopelessness, shame, depression, hurt, anxiety, and fear. Let your emotions draw you into my presence so that I can align your inner world with my truth and lead you safely out of the storm.

Surrender to God's Way

In this time of prayer pause to discover the emotions your heart holds. (See the emotions journal in appendix to assist you.) Sit with them awhile and watch as God walks right in to meet you there. Whatever it is. Whether it be despair, hopelessness, fear, depression, grief, anger, shame, bitterness, let him shed his light on those hurting places and show you the way out. He promises not to leave you there. Maybe your heart is overflowing with excitement, hope, joy, or gratefulness. He wants to meet you there too and celebrate every emotion-filled moment with you!

Give God the space and time to expose any limiting mindsets (things you speak or believe) and protective strategies (things you do) that are hindering you from connecting with your inner world and experiencing God's presence no matter the weather. Break the power of any belief or strategy's hold over you by asking God to forgive you for partnering with views and actions that don't line up with his truth!

Write your own personal prayer of surrender here:

_____

_____

_____

_____

_____

_____

_____

_____

_____

_____

_____

_____

_____

_____

_____

Expect God to Move on My Behalf

Expect God to hear the cries of your heart. God wants all of you—even the emotions you are ashamed to admit exist in you. Let his presence reset your soul and lead you to steady ground once again.

Visualize a truth-filled thought based on what God revealed to your heart today and renew your mind in it all day long. Speak it, repeat it, be it!

My truth-focused thought for today:

_____

_____

Pause, Sit and Soak In His Presence

Sit and soak in the beauty of what God revealed to your heart today. Grant yourself the freedom to visualize fully and creatively express the thoughts, impressions, or images that come to your mind in any format that is best for you. Write, draw, paint, or collage allowing the images and words to flow freely from your heart so that your eyes can capture hope for the journey.

Mining Deeper

To mine is to dig deep and uncover treasures once hidden. It requires a search with the eyes and a heart that hungers for more. It is a willingness to explore unknown territory while trusting in the One leading the way. Over the course of the next few days, weeks, and months watch for how God continues to unfold deeper layers of truth regarding the area he spotlighted in your heart today. He rarely uncovers every layer all at once, because more than anything he wants daily intimacy with you. He wants you to mine the depths of his heart and as you do, he will uncover treasures before your eyes that will lead you to greater levels of freedom. Come back to this space to record and make note of the treasures he is leading your heart to discover!

Fill your thoughts with my words until they penetrate deep into your spirit. Then as you unwrap my words, they will impart true life and radiant health into the very core of your being.

Proverbs 4:21-22 (TPT)

Mining Topic: The place in my heart in need of God's view.

My God-Directed Discoveries:

Day 18 Your Mindsets

Thought of the day: Your thoughts are either your source of victory or defeat. You get to choose!

I will CEASE today by choosing to:

Connect with God

Daily Word

Romans 12:2 (NLT)

Don't copy the behavior and customs of this world, but let God transform you into a new person by changing the way you think. Then you will learn to know God's will for you, which is good and pleasing and perfect.

Daily Worship

"Resurrecting" by Elevation Worship

Note here how this verse and song spoke directly to your heart:

_____

_____

_____

_____

_____

_____

_____

_____

_____

Examine My Heart

What would your self-portrait look like if your thoughts were painting it? In what direction are your thoughts leading you? Pause to notice what you are speaking over your life and your future. Ask God to reveal to you limiting mindsets that are paralyzing the destiny he has designed specifically for you to fulfill.

_____

_____

_____

_____

Allow God to Open My Heart to His View

You cannot change anything until you change the way you think. If your thoughts do not align with my truth they will always lead you astray. I want you to see what I see and know what I know. Seek me first—always! I will transform you by placing my thoughts within you. I want you to know my heart for you, my hopes for you, my dreams for you, and how beautiful you are to me! Get alone with my thoughts for you and they will set you free! Consume me and my truths daily. Too many distractions and lies are thrown your way every hour of the day. The enemy will target your mind the most. If he can plant seeds within you that don't line up with how I see you, he can make you doubt everything I want to do through you. Align your heart and mind with mine. Let my Word be ever before you—leading your coming and your going. I promise you that as you get your thoughts in line with mine you will experience victory, and my dreams for you will come to life!

Surrender to God's Way

In this time of prayer seek God's truth for every lie you have been believing about yourself, God, and the future he has for you. Give God the space and time to expose any limiting mindsets (things you speak or believe) and protective strategies (things you do) that are hindering you from accepting his truth in your heart. Break the power of any belief or strategy's hold over you by asking God to forgive you for partnering with views and actions that don't line up with his truth!

Write your own personal prayer of surrender here:

_____

_____

_____

_____

_____

_____

_____

_____

_____

_____

_____

_____

_____

_____

Expect God to Move on My Behalf

Expect God's Truth to set you free! Align your thoughts with his so that he can take you places you never thought you could go!

Visualize a truth-filled thought based on what God revealed to your heart today and renew your mind in it all day long. Speak it, repeat it, be it!

My truth-focused thought for today:

_____

_____

Pause, Sit and Soak In His Presence

Sit and soak in the beauty of what God revealed to your heart today. Grant yourself the freedom to visualize fully and creatively express the thoughts, impressions, or images that come to your mind in any format that is best for you. Write, draw, paint, or collage allowing the images and words to flow freely from your heart so that your eyes can capture hope for the journey.

Mining Deeper

To mine is to dig deep and uncover treasures once hidden. It requires a search with the eyes and a heart that hungers for more. It is a willingness to explore unknown territory while trusting in the One leading the way. Over the course of the next few days, weeks, and months watch for how God continues to unfold deeper layers of truth regarding the area he spotlighted in your heart today. He rarely uncovers every layer all at once, because more than anything he wants daily intimacy with you. He wants you to mine the depths of his heart and as you do, he will uncover treasures before your eyes that will lead you to greater levels of freedom. Come back to this space to record and make note of the treasures he is leading your heart to discover!

Fill your thoughts with my words until they penetrate deep into your spirit. Then as you unwrap my words, they will impart true life and radiant health into the very core of your being.

Proverbs 4:21-22 (TPT)

Mining Topic: The place in my heart in need of God's view.

My God-Directed Discoveries:

Day 19 Your Protective Strategies

Thought of the day: Letting go of control opens our hearts to experience God's path for our lives.

I will CEASE today by choosing to:

Connect with God

Daily Word

Proverbs 3: 5-6 (NLT)

Trust in the Lord with all your heart; do not depend on your own understanding. Seek his will in all you do, and he will show you which path to take.

Daily Worship

"My Heart Is Yours" by Kristian Stanfill of Passion

Note here how this verse and song spoke directly to your heart:

_____

_____

_____

_____

_____

_____

_____

Examine My Heart

In the moments that you felt betrayed, crushed, and overwhelmed, what self-promises did you etch into your heart? What's the first phrase that comes to mind when you see the words, "I'll never...?" What protective strategies did you devise so that you would never have to feel vulnerable again? Ask God to reveal to you the places where you have grabbed the reins and struggle to let him have control.

_____

_____

_____

_____

Allow God to Open My Heart to His View

There have been times that your heart was broken, overwhelmed, in despair and you promised yourself "*Never again*". Those promises and ways you have protected yourself have blocked what I want to give you now. I know you feel I let you down and I didn't come through for you but that has never been the case. I can be trusted with your heart again. All that I am is for you, even when this life stings. Let me light up the path of freedom before you. For I know how to turn your every experience into strength and your every battle into a resiliency that cannot be stolen. I want to help you navigate the road ahead, but you must open your heart to trust me and my promises for you. I get that life hasn't always made sense and at times has totally blindsided you. So, you did what you thought was best at the time, but now let me show you a better way. With your heart in my hands, I can be your refuge, your guide, and your limitless supply of grace. I can't promise you that you will never experience more hurt in this fallen world, but I can promise you that nothing that comes your way will defeat you or overtake you with your heart in my hands. I have sealed you with my Spirit. Let me equip you and place my armor upon you so that you will know how to face any battle. What I need from you now is to lay down your way for mine so that I can prove to you my way is perfect and my heart is kind!

Surrender to God's Way

In this time of prayer seek God's strategies for your life. Let him be the guard at your gate and the guide to your heart. Lay down your self-protective strategies so that God can direct your way! Give God the space and time to expose any limiting mindsets (things you speak or believe) and protective strategies (things you do) that are hindering you from letting go and giving him control. Break the power of any belief or strategy's hold over you by asking God to forgive you for partnering with views and actions that don't line up with his truth!

Write your own personal prayer of surrender here:

_____

_____

_____

_____

_____

_____

_____

_____

_____

_____

Expect God to Move on My Behalf

Expect God's way and his promises to guide you to the path of freedom and wholeness you long for. Let go of your way so God's can begin!

Visualize a truth-filled thought based on what God revealed to your heart today and renew your mind in it all day long. Speak it, repeat it, be it!

My truth-focused thought for today:

_____

_____

Pause, Sit and Soak In His Presence

Sit and soak in the beauty of what God revealed to your heart today. Grant yourself the freedom to visualize fully and creatively express the thoughts, impressions, or images that come to your mind in any format that is best for you. Write, draw, paint, or collage allowing the images and words to flow freely from your heart so that your eyes can capture hope for the journey.

Mining Deeper

To mine is to dig deep and uncover treasures once hidden. It requires a search with the eyes and a heart that hungers for more. It is a willingness to explore unknown territory while trusting in the One leading the way. Over the course of the next few days, weeks, and months watch for how God continues to unfold deeper layers of truth regarding the area he spotlighted in your heart today. He rarely uncovers every layer all at once, because more than anything he wants daily intimacy with you. He wants you to mine the depths of his heart and as you do, he will uncover treasures before your eyes that will lead you to greater levels of freedom. Come back to this space to record and make note of the treasures he is leading your heart to discover!

Fill your thoughts with my words until they penetrate deep into your spirit. Then as you unwrap my words, they will impart true life and radiant health into the very core of your being.

Proverbs 4:21-22 (TPT)

Mining Topic: The place in my heart in need of God's view.

_____

My God-Directed Discoveries:

_____

_____

_____

_____

_____

_____

_____

_____

_____

_____

_____

_____

_____

_____

_____

Day 20 Tucked-Away Places

Thought of the day: God cannot heal the places you're too afraid to let his light shine in.

I will CEASE today by choosing to:

Connect with God

Daily Word

Matthew 13:15 (NIV)

For this people's heart has become calloused; they hardly hear with their ears, and they have closed their eyes. Otherwise they might see with their eyes, hear with their ears, understand with their hearts and turn, and I would heal them.

Daily Worship

"Sails" by Pat Barrett & Steffany Gretzinger

Note here how this verse and song spoke directly to your heart:

_____

_____

_____

_____

_____

_____

_____

_____

Examine My Heart

Are there places in your heart that have been so devastated by life that you've completely tucked them away letting no one else see? Ask God to reveal to you the tender places within that are most in need of his touch.

_____

_____

_____

_____

_____

_____

Allow God to Open My Heart to His View

I have seen it all—nothing is hidden from my eyes. You don't have to say a word, I know the thoughts that keep you up at night and the fears that steal your peace. I care deeply about the devastation in your heart and the burdens you have been carrying. You don't have to face this alone. I want to redefine how you have viewed the painful moments of your life and give you a completely new perspective. Let me fill the places shame has resided within you with my love, grace, and acceptance. No child of mine is to live shamed. Even if you feel it is the worst sin ever committed, whatever you open before me, I can purify, heal, and set you free. The places you have kept tucked away, I cannot enter. Freedom is yours—my free-gift to you paid in full by my Cross. Let my grace breathe on the sails of your heart and set you free! I have so many places I want you to see and experience. Let's explore together and sail on new waters—leaving the past behind.

Surrender to God's Way

In this time of prayer hear God calling your name, nothing between you and him, nothing hidden. Let him flood your walls and watch as his love, grace, and mercy wash in and relieve you of all shame. Give God the space and time to expose any limiting mindsets (things you speak or believe) and protective strategies (things you do) that are causing you to hide parts of your story away. Break the power of any belief or strategy's hold over you by asking God to forgive you for partnering with views and actions that don't line up with his truth!

Write your own personal prayer of surrender here:

_____

_____

_____

_____

_____

_____

_____

_____

_____

_____

_____

Expect God to Move on My Behalf

Expect God's grace to be enough for you. Know that nothing is beyond his ability to heal. Including, the deepest, darkest places in your heart you want no one to see. As you open all of your heart to him, he will embrace you, accept you, and restore all the broken places within you.

Visualize a truth-filled thought based on what God revealed to your heart today and renew your mind in it all day long. Speak it, repeat it, be it!

My truth-focused thought for today:

_____

_____

Pause, Sit and Soak In His Presence

Sit and soak in the beauty of what God revealed to your heart today. Grant yourself the freedom to visualize fully and creatively express the thoughts, impressions, or images that come to your mind in any format that is best for you. Write, draw, paint, or collage allowing the images and words to flow freely from your heart so that your eyes can capture hope for the journey.

Mining Deeper

To mine is to dig deep and uncover treasures once hidden. It requires a search with the eyes and a heart that hungers for more. It is a willingness to explore unknown territory while trusting in the One leading the way. Over the course of the next few days, weeks, and months watch for how God continues to unfold deeper layers of truth regarding the area he spotlighted in your heart today. He rarely uncovers every layer all at once, because more than anything he wants daily intimacy with you. He wants you to mine the depths of his heart and as you do, he will uncover treasures before your eyes that will lead you to greater levels of freedom. Come back to this space to record and make note of the treasures he is leading your heart to discover!

Fill your thoughts with my words until they penetrate deep into your spirit. Then as you unwrap my words, they will impart true life and radiant health into the very core of your being.

Proverbs 4:21-22 (TPT)

Mining Topic: The place in my heart in need of God's view.

_____

My God-Directed Discoveries:

_____

_____

_____

_____

_____

_____

_____

_____

_____

_____

_____

_____

_____

_____

Day 21 The Labels You've Accepted

Thought of the day: The God who created you is the only one with the right to tell you who you are!

I will CEASE today by choosing to:

Connect with God

Daily Word

Isaiah 43:1 (NIV)

But now, this is what the LORD says—he who created you, Jacob, he who formed you, Israel: "Do not fear, for I have redeemed you; I have summoned you by name; you are mine."

Daily Worship

"Hello, My Name Is" by Matthew West

Note here how this verse and song spoke directly to your heart:

_____

_____

_____

_____

_____

_____

_____

Examine My Heart

Negative words spoken over us can become sticky like tar and hard to shake off. Who currently holds the power over how you view yourself most? Ask God to reveal to you any damaging words spoken over you that are causing you to reject the words God wants to speak into your heart about who you really are.

_____

_____

_____

_____

Allow God to Open My Heart to His View

Negative labels cripple the soul. I want to replace any false names spoken over you with my truth. I have seen your heart shatter when others have been harsh, unloving, and cruel. They spoke things over you that were a projection of the hurt in their hearts, and it spilled onto you. Release the hold these harsh words, negative perceptions, and false labels have had on you and let me paint the true picture of who you are on the canvas of your heart. These negative labels are holding you back and I want to move you forward. I have so much for you to see and do, and you can't do it if you remain stuck in the past with labels that are blurring your view. Unzip and step out of the false picture other's hurtful words created in your heart so that you can step into the light of who you were meant to be all along!

Surrender to God's Way

In this time of prayer imagine yourself tearing off *any and all* negative labels placed on you by others and let the true name giver repaint the inner canvas of your heart with how he sees you. Give God the space and time to expose any limiting mindsets (things you speak or believe) and protective strategies (things you do) that are hindering your ability to accept the new labels God wants to give you. Break the power of any belief or strategy's hold over you by asking God to forgive you for partnering with views and actions that don't line up with his truth!

Write your own personal prayer of surrender here:

_____

_____

_____

_____

_____

_____

_____

_____

_____

_____

_____

_____

_____

_____

_____

Expect God to Move on My Behalf

Expect God to rename you and reclaim you because he has a destiny to prepare you for!

Visualize a truth-filled thought based on what God revealed to your heart today and renew your mind in it all day long. Speak it, repeat it, be it!

My truth-focused thought for today:

_____

_____

Pause, Sit and Soak In His Presence

Sit and soak in the beauty of what God revealed to your heart today. Grant yourself the freedom to visualize fully and creatively express the thoughts, impressions, or images that come to your mind in any format that is best for you. Write, draw, paint, or collage allowing the images and words to flow freely from your heart so that your eyes can capture hope for the journey.

Mining Deeper

To mine is to dig deep and uncover treasures once hidden. It requires a search with the eyes and a heart that hungers for more. It is a willingness to explore unknown territory while trusting in the One leading the way. Over the course of the next few days, weeks, and months watch for how God continues to unfold deeper layers of truth regarding the area he spotlighted in your heart today. He rarely uncovers every layer all at once, because more than anything he wants daily intimacy with you. He wants you to mine the depths of his heart and as you do, he will uncover treasures before your eyes that will lead you to greater levels of freedom. Come back to this space to record and make note of the treasures he is leading your heart to discover!

Fill your thoughts with my words until they penetrate deep into your spirit. Then as you unwrap my words, they will impart true life and radiant health into the very core of your being.

Proverbs 4:21-22 (TPT)

Mining Topic: The place in my heart in need of God's view.

_____

My God-Directed Discoveries:

Day 22 The Hope Within You

Thought of the day: Change is possible because of the power of Christ within you!

I will CEASE today by choosing to:

Connect with God

Daily Word

Hebrews 10:22-23 (TPT)

For our hearts have been sprinkled with blood to remove impurity and we have been freed from an accusing conscience and now we are clean, unstained, and presentable to God inside and out! So now we must cling tightly to the hope that lives within us, knowing that God always keeps his promises!

Daily Worship

"Different" by Micah Tyler

Note here how this verse and song spoke directly to your heart:

_____

_____

_____

_____

_____

_____

_____

_____

Examine My Heart

Do you believe that change, healing, and freedom are possible for you? Ask God to show you the power he has placed within you to transform you, reshape you, and refine you into his images.

_____

_____

_____

_____

_____

Allow God to Open My Heart to His View

I have a new "You" to prepare you for. You won't even recognize yourself with I am through. Place your hope in me alone. I will lead you through a process of change. Don't grow weary with the time true transformation takes. I promise to see it through to the end. I want any change that takes place within you to become permanent. Don't give up! There will be painful moments in letting go but I promise it is worth the freedom that is waiting for you on the other side. My Spirit within you is a transforming power that nothing can stop once it is set in motion. Believe and have confidence in my promises to refine you, shape you, and mold you into my image. I want to set you free from anything that holds you back. I can't wait for you to experience the freedom I want to give you. Your heart will leap with joy, peace, and confidence. Let's do this! Now is your time to let go of everything that hinders you and run your race!

Surrender to God's Way

In this time of prayer let hope rise within you as you look forward to the road of transformation ahead of you. Believe that God's presence within you will leave you forever changed! Give God the space and time to expose any limiting mindsets (things you speak or believe) and protective strategies (things you do) that are hindering you from believing in God's ability to transform you from the inside out. Break the power of any belief or strategy's hold over you by asking God to forgive you for partnering with views and actions that don't line up with his truth!

Write your own personal prayer of surrender here:

_____

_____

_____

_____

_____

_____

_____

_____

_____

_____

_____

_____

_____

Expect God to Move on My Behalf

Expect God's presence to forever change you. A new "You" is beginning to take shape!

Visualize a truth-filled thought based on what God revealed to your heart today and renew your mind in it all day long. Speak it, repeat it, be it!

My truth-focused thought for today:

_____

_____

Pause, Sit and Soak In His Presence

Sit and soak in the beauty of what God revealed to your heart today. Grant yourself the freedom to visualize fully and creatively express the thoughts, impressions, or images that come to your mind in any format that is best for you. Write, draw, paint, or collage allowing the images and words to flow freely from your heart so that your eyes can capture hope for the journey.

Mining Deeper

To mine is to dig deep and uncover treasures once hidden. It requires a search with the eyes and a heart that hungers for more. It is a willingness to explore unknown territory while trusting in the One leading the way. Over the course of the next few days, weeks, and months watch for how God continues to unfold deeper layers of truth regarding the area he spotlighted in your heart today. He rarely uncovers every layer all at once, because more than anything he wants daily intimacy with you. He wants you to mine the depths of his heart and as you do, he will uncover treasures before your eyes that will lead you to greater levels of freedom. Come back to this space to record and make note of the treasures he is leading your heart to discover!

Fill your thoughts with my words until they penetrate deep into your spirit. Then as you unwrap my words, they will impart true life and radiant health into the very core of your being.

Proverbs 4:21-22 (TPT)

Mining Topic: The place in my heart in need of God's view.

My God-Directed Discoveries:

Experience Freedom

Day 23 Your True Identity—God's View of You

Thought of the day: I am made new in Christ. The old is gone and the new has come!

I will CEASE today by choosing to:

Connect with God

Daily Word

2 Corinthians 5:17 (ESV)

Therefore, if anyone is in Christ, he is a new creation. The old has passed away; behold, the new has come.

Daily Worship

"You Define Me" by Kim Walker-Smith

Note here how this verse and song spoke directly to your heart:

_____

_____

_____

_____

_____

_____

_____

_____

Examine My Heart

What have I been believing about my identity that does not line up with the truth in God's Word? Have I been believing lies that tell me: "I'm not enough", "I'm unworthy", "I'm broken, damaged, and a failure"? Lord, reveal to my heart who you say that I am!

_____

_____

_____

_____

_____

Allow God to Open My Heart to His View

My heart adores you and I cannot wait to tell you who you are. You are beautiful to me. A masterpiece of all masterpieces. I designed you specifically. I carefully planned every detail— from the color of your eyes, to the heart you possess, and all the way down to the tip of your toes. I gladly claim you as my own unique design. You are loved! You are cherished! You are my treasure, my delight. I have made you completely new. No trace of the past. You lack nothing, and you are worthy of the dreams I have for you. I created you just the way you are so that you could accomplish the specific plans I have designed for your life. Within your heart I placed my power, my might, all that I am. You are my warrior, my nothing-can-stop-you, conqueror! You are gifted, you are full of grace, you are ready for the tasks ahead of you. I know you. I love you. I can't wait for you to see yourself through my eyes because what I see just blows me away.

Surrender to God's Way

In this time of prayer ask God to help you see yourself through his eyes. Give God the space and time to expose any limiting mindsets (things you speak or believe) and protective strategies (things you do) that are hindering you from accepting your true-identity in Christ. Break the power of any belief or strategy's hold over you by asking God to forgive you for partnering with views and actions that don't line up with his truth!

Write your own personal prayer of surrender here:

_____

_____

_____

_____

_____

_____

_____

_____

_____

_____

_____

_____

_____

Expect God to Move on My Behalf

Expect God to be blown away by you! He can't get enough of you. Open your heart to see yourself through his eyes. He has the best view around.

Visualize a truth-filled thought based on what God revealed to your heart today and renew your mind in it all day long. Speak it, repeat it, be it!

My truth-focused thought for today:

_____

_____

Pause, Sit and Soak In His Presence

Sit and soak in the beauty of what God revealed to your heart today. Grant yourself the freedom to visualize fully and creatively express the thoughts, impressions, or images that come to your mind in any format that is best for you. Write, draw, paint, or collage allowing the images and words to flow freely from your heart so that your eyes can capture hope for the journey.

Mining Deeper

To mine is to dig deep and uncover treasures once hidden. It requires a search with the eyes and a heart that hungers for more. It is a willingness to explore unknown territory while trusting in the One leading the way. Over the course of the next few days, weeks, and months watch for how God continues to unfold deeper layers of truth regarding the area he spotlighted in your heart today. He rarely uncovers every layer all at once, because more than anything he wants daily intimacy with you. He wants you to mine the depths of his heart and as you do, he will uncover treasures before your eyes that will lead you to greater levels of freedom. Come back to this space to record and make note of the treasures he is leading your heart to discover!

Fill your thoughts with my words until they penetrate deep into your spirit. Then as you unwrap my words, they will impart true life and radiant health into the very core of your being.

Proverbs 4:21-22 (TPT)

Mining Topic: The place in my heart in need of God's view.

_____

My God-Directed Discoveries:

_____

_____

_____

_____

_____

_____

_____

_____

_____

_____

_____

_____

_____

_____

Day 24 Self-Forgiveness

Thought of the day: God's arms are open wide.

I will CEASE today by choosing to:

Connect with God

Daily Word

Psalm 103: 3 (TPT)

You kissed my heart with forgiveness, in spite of all I've done. You've healed me inside and out from every disease.

Daily Worship

"O Come to the Altar" by Elevation Worship

Note here how this verse and song spoke directly to your heart:

_____

_____

_____

_____

_____

_____

_____

Examine My Heart

What are you holding against yourself and can't seem to forgive yourself for? What haunts your heart? Ask God to reveal to you the places where you need to extend forgiveness to yourself.

_____

_____

_____

_____

_____

_____

Allow God to Open My Heart to His View

Come to me; lay your face at the altar of my grace. My arms are open wide. What you lay at my feet I release as far as the east is from the west and remember it no more. When you hold unforgiveness towards yourself in your heart, my grace cannot enter. My grace *is enough!* It covers everything—every slip up, every mistake, every shame-filled moment. Nothing is beyond its reach! When you accept my gift of grace in your heart, it is the most freeing experience you will ever know. I see you as pure, clean, and white before me because my Cross doesn't allow me to see anything different. Let go. Let go. Let go. Forgive yourself because I already have. I sacrificed my life so that I could take your place and wrap you in my righteousness. You are free, but you have to *believe* you are! Accept my free-gift of grace. I want your heart free of shame and condemnation. When you walk in self-love, loving yourself as I have loved you, you can conqueror anything. Your inner love will spill out into the world and become a powerful river that will flow continuously and be unstoppable. Forgive yourself and accept my grace. It is yours for the taking!

Surrender to God's Way

In this time of prayer lay yourself at God's feet and pour out your heart to him. Set yourself free from the things you are holding against yourself by accepting his free-gift of grace into your heart. Give God the space and time to expose any limiting mindsets (things you speak or believe) and protective strategies (things you do) that are hindering you from being able to let yourself off the hook and accept God's grace. Break the power of any belief or strategy's hold over you by asking God to forgive you for partnering with views and actions that don't line up with his truth!

Write your own personal prayer of surrender here:

_____

_____

_____

_____

_____

_____

_____

_____

_____

_____

Expect God to Move on My Behalf

Expect to be forgiven and set free! Nothing is beyond God's grace. Jesus' sacrifice leaves no room for shame.

Visualize a truth-filled thought based on what God revealed to your heart today and renew your mind in it all day long. Speak it, repeat it, be it!

My truth-focused thought for today:

_____

_____

Pause, Sit and Soak In His Presence

Sit and soak in the beauty of what God revealed to your heart today. Grant yourself the freedom to visualize fully and creatively express the thoughts, impressions, or images that come to your mind in any format that is best for you. Write, draw, paint, or collage allowing the images and words to flow freely from your heart so that your eyes can capture hope for the journey.

Mining Deeper

To mine is to dig deep and uncover treasures once hidden. It requires a search with the eyes and a heart that hungers for more. It is a willingness to explore unknown territory while trusting in the One leading the way. Over the course of the next few days, weeks, and months watch for how God continues to unfold deeper layers of truth regarding the area he spotlighted in your heart today. He rarely uncovers every layer all at once, because more than anything he wants daily intimacy with you. He wants you to mine the depths of his heart and as you do, he will uncover treasures before your eyes that will lead you to greater levels of freedom. Come back to this space to record and make note of the treasures he is leading your heart to discover!

Fill your thoughts with my words until they penetrate deep into your spirit. Then as you unwrap my words, they will impart true life and radiant health into the very core of your being.

Proverbs 4:21-22 (TPT)

Mining Topic: The place in my heart in need of God's view.

_____

My God-Directed Discoveries:

_____

_____

_____

_____

_____

_____

_____

_____

_____

_____

_____

_____

_____

_____

Day 25 Forgiving Others

Thought of the day: What you won't let go of, won't let go of you!

I will CEASE today by choosing to:

Connect with God

Daily Word

Colossians 3:13-14 (MSG)

So, chosen by God for this new life of love, dress in the wardrobe God picked out for you: compassion, kindness, humility, quiet strength, discipline. Be even-tempered, content with second place, quick to forgive an offense. Forgive as quickly and completely as the Master forgave you. And regardless of what else you put on, wear love. It's your basic, all-purpose garment. Never be without it.

Daily Worship

"Forgiveness" by Matthew West

Note here how this verse and song spoke directly to your heart:

_____

_____

_____

_____

_____

_____

Examine My Heart

We are all broken in our own way. Hurting hearts—hurt others. Shamed hearts—shame others, but hope-filled hearts fill others with hope, and grace-filled hearts spill grace onto others! What do you want to spread? Are there places in your heart so full of hurt, wounded by other people's actions, that you struggle to forgive? Ask God to reveal to you the places that are keeping you chained to your past because of unforgiveness.

_____

_____

_____

_____

Allow God to Open My Heart to His View

This world is full of hurting people in need of my grace. Unhealed hearts can do some major damage to those around them. I know you got caught in the cross-fire of their pain and ended up deeply wounded. But holding on just keeps the pain festering. Forgiving isn't about them—it is *your* key to freedom. Forgiveness clears your heart from the chains of your past and allows my perspective to sink deeply into those wounded places. Holding on as if it protects you is a false sense of security that only results in being enslaved to fear. I know it hurts, but the longer you hold on, the longer your freedom must wait. I don't want anything but my love to consume your heart. Bitterness spreads and becomes like a cancer that robs you of joy and peace. Bring your hurt to me and I promise to help you set it free.

Surrender to God's Way

In this time of prayer lay your raw hurting heart before God and let him place a healing salve on your wounds. Ask God to show you the person(s) you are struggling to forgive through his eyes and begin the process of extending forgiveness to them so that you can be free from the past. Give God the space and time to expose any limiting mindsets (things you speak or believe) and protective strategies (things you do) that are hindering you from letting go and forgiving those who hurt and wounded you. Break the power of any belief or strategy's hold over you by asking God to forgive you for partnering with views and actions that don't line up with his truth!

Write your own personal prayer of surrender here:

_____

_____

_____

_____

_____

_____

_____

_____

_____

_____

_____

_____

_____

Expect God to Move on My Behalf

Expect chains to fall off you and freedom to flood your heart when you let go of the hurt others have caused you. God has your back. Let go and be free!

Visualize a truth-filled thought based on what God revealed to your heart today and renew your mind in it all day long. Speak it, repeat it, be it!

My truth-focused thought for today:

_____

_____

Pause, Sit and Soak In His Presence

Sit and soak in the beauty of what God revealed to your heart today. Grant yourself the freedom to visualize fully and creatively express the thoughts, impressions, or images that come to your mind in any format that is best for you. Write, draw, paint, or collage allowing the images and words to flow freely from your heart so that your eyes can capture hope for the journey.

Mining Deeper

To mine is to dig deep and uncover treasures once hidden. It requires a search with the eyes and a heart that hungers for more. It is a willingness to explore unknown territory while trusting in the One leading the way. Over the course of the next few days, weeks, and months watch for how God continues to unfold deeper layers of truth regarding the area he spotlighted in your heart today. He rarely uncovers every layer all at once, because more than anything he wants daily intimacy with you. He wants you to mine the depths of his heart and as you do, he will uncover treasures before your eyes that will lead you to greater levels of freedom. Come back to this space to record and make note of the treasures he is leading your heart to discover!

Fill your thoughts with my words until they penetrate deep into your spirit. Then as you unwrap my words, they will impart true life and radiant health into the very core of your being.

Proverbs 4:21-22 (TPT)

Mining Topic: The place in my heart in need of God's view.

_____

My God-Directed Discoveries:

_____

_____

_____

_____

_____

_____

_____

_____

_____

_____

_____

_____

_____

_____

_____

_____

Day 26 Forgiving God

Thought of the day: God's thoughts about you are always pure and for your good.

I will CEASE today by choosing to:

Connect with God

Daily Word

Psalm 139: 17-18 (TPT)

Every single moment you are thinking of me! How precious and wonderful to consider that you cherish me constantly in your every thought! O God, your desires towards me are more than the grains of sand on every shore! When I awake each morning, you're still with me.

Daily Worship

"Even If" by Mercy Me

Note here how this verse and song spoke directly to your heart:

_____

_____

_____

_____

_____

_____

_____

_____

Examine My Heart

Are their places in your heart you feel God has let you down or abandoned you? Do you feel like God doesn't care about you or answer your prayers in the way he does for others? Ask God to reveal any places in your heart where you are struggling to forgive him for things that have happened to you or places where you felt he didn't provide.

_____

_____

_____

_____

Allow God to Open My Heart to His View

I know you may think I let you down and wasn't there for you. I've given every person the right to choose love, but some don't choose me. My way is always love! The enemy tries hard to lie to you about who I really am! Separation from me helps his plans succeed. This life will bring pain, sorrow, and moments you don't understand. I promise to be your refuge in the storm, because the storms will come. Trust me to lead you safely through the storms you face. I know your heart struggles to comprehend it, but my thoughts for you are so much greater than you could ever imagine. I am always seeking to develop you more and more into my image. Let me use the circumstances of your life to create a light in you that burns so brightly nothing can stop it. You are here to be a light—a light of hope, compassion, and encouragement for others. Victory in your storm turns into victory for others. It is all about connection. The enemy seeks to disconnect me to my people and my people to each other because there is no force on earth greater than love. Love expressed no matter what life presents will always conquer. Let no circumstance rob you of your freedom to love and be loved!

Surrender to God's Way

In this time of prayer be honest with God about the times you felt he let you down. Give God the space and time to expose any limiting mindsets (things you speak or believe) and protective strategies (things you do) that are hindering your ability to forgive God and trust in his ultimate plan. Break the power of any belief or strategy's hold over you by asking God to forgive you for partnering with views and actions that don't line up with his truth!

Write your own personal prayer of surrender here:

_____

_____

_____

_____

_____

_____

_____

_____

_____

_____

_____

Expect God to Move on My Behalf

Expect every seemingly unanswered prayer to be lace with God's love and goodness and that every storm is an opportunity to be transformed more and more into his image!

Visualize a truth-filled thought based on what God revealed to your heart today and renew your mind in it all day long. Speak it, repeat it, be it!

My truth-focused thought for today:

_____

_____

Pause, Sit and Soak In His Presence

Sit and soak in the beauty of what God revealed to your heart today. Grant yourself the freedom to visualize fully and creatively express the thoughts, impressions, or images that come to your mind in any format that is best for you. Write, draw, paint, or collage allowing the images and words to flow freely from your heart so that your eyes can capture hope for the journey.

Mining Deeper

To mine is to dig deep and uncover treasures once hidden. It requires a search with the eyes and a heart that hungers for more. It is a willingness to explore unknown territory while trusting in the One leading the way. Over the course of the next few days, weeks, and months watch for how God continues to unfold deeper layers of truth regarding the area he spotlighted in your heart today. He rarely uncovers every layer all at once, because more than anything he wants daily intimacy with you. He wants you to mine the depths of his heart and as you do, he will uncover treasures before your eyes that will lead you to greater levels of freedom. Come back to this space to record and make note of the treasures he is leading your heart to discover!

Fill your thoughts with my words until they penetrate deep into your spirit. Then as you unwrap my words, they will impart true life and radiant health into the very core of your being.

Proverbs 4:21-22 (TPT)

Mining Topic: The place in my heart in need of God's view.

My God-Directed Discoveries:

Day 27 Making Amends

Thought of the day: Humility is a beautiful gift we extend to others that never goes unnoticed by God.

I will CEASE today by choosing to:

Connect with God

Daily Word

1 Peter 5:5-6 (NLT)

And all of you, dress yourselves in humility as you relate to one another, for God opposes the proud but gives grace to the humble. So humble yourselves under the mighty power of God, and at the right time he will lift you up in honor.

Daily Worship

"Broken Vessels" by Hillsong

Note here how this verse and song spoke directly to your heart:

_____

_____

_____

_____

_____

_____

_____

_____

Examine My Heart

Are there places you need to admit your faults and look honestly at where you have wronged others? Have there been times you let your hurt fuel your actions and others got burned? Ask God to reveal to your heart anyone to whom you may need to seek their forgiveness and admit where you have been wrong.

_____

_____

_____

_____

Allow God to Open My Heart to His View

Free others by being courageous enough to be open about your faults, weaknesses, and struggles. I have never expected you to be perfect, but I do expect you to be authentic, genuine, and kind. Be humble enough to bring restoration where you can. Shower mercy and grace on others and accept yourself in your mistakes. Let my love propel you to connect fully with others. Live an offense-free life—forgiving others of their mistakes and seeking forgiveness for yours. You're all in the same boat—in need of my grace. Seek to speak words of life and encouragement into the hearts of those around you. See the best in others and speak over them the potential I see in them. Accept others in their messy places and spread love and mercy everywhere you go. There is no greater gift than the gift of my love that flows from a humble heart.

Surrender to God's Way

In this time of prayer, humble yourself and genuinely search your heart for actions you've taken or words you have spoken that you need to make right. Humility is the antidote to hate and places the enemy beneath our feet where he belongs. Give God the space and time to expose any limiting mindsets (things you speak or believe) and protective strategies (things you do) that are hindering your ability to look honestly at your faults and make amends where possible. Break the power of any belief or strategy's hold over you by asking God to forgive you for partnering with views and actions that don't line up with his truth!

Write your own personal prayer of surrender here:

_____

_____

_____

_____

_____

_____

_____

_____

_____

_____

_____

_____

Expect God to Move on My Behalf

Expect God to honor your humility. When you are real, genuine, and vulnerable, it frees others to do the same!

Visualize a truth-filled thought based on what God revealed to your heart today and renew your mind in it all day long. Speak it, repeat it, be it!

My truth-focused thought for today:

_____

_____

Pause, Sit and Soak In His Presence

Sit and soak in the beauty of what God revealed to your heart today. Grant yourself the freedom to visualize fully and creatively express the thoughts, impressions, or images that come to your mind in any format that is best for you. Write, draw, paint, or collage allowing the images and words to flow freely from your heart so that your eyes can capture hope for the journey.

Mining Deeper

To mine is to dig deep and uncover treasures once hidden. It requires a search with the eyes and a heart that hungers for more. It is a willingness to explore unknown territory while trusting in the One leading the way. Over the course of the next few days, weeks, and months watch for how God continues to unfold deeper layers of truth regarding the area he spotlighted in your heart today. He rarely uncovers every layer all at once, because more than anything he wants daily intimacy with you. He wants you to mine the depths of his heart and as you do, he will uncover treasures before your eyes that will lead you to greater levels of freedom. Come back to this space to record and make note of the treasures he is leading your heart to discover!

Fill your thoughts with my words until they penetrate deep into your spirit. Then as you unwrap my words, they will impart true life and radiant health into the very core of your being.

Proverbs 4:21-22 (TPT)

Mining Topic: The place in my heart in need of God's view.

_____

My God-Directed Discoveries:

_____

_____

_____

_____

_____

_____

_____

_____

_____

_____

_____

_____

_____

_____

_____

_____

Day 28 Breaking Free

Thought of the day: God's truth sets us free!

I will CEASE today by choosing to:

Connect with God

Daily Word

Psalm 118:5–6 (NLT)

In my distress I prayed to the Lord, and the Lord answered me and set me free. The Lord is for me, so I will have no fear.

Daily Worship

"Glorious Day" by Kristian Stanfill of Passion

Note here how this verse and song spoke directly to your heart:

_____

_____

_____

_____

_____

_____

_____

_____

Examine My Heart

What does your heart need to break free from? During this journey what has been the resounding message God has been bringing to your awareness? He does this because he knows that the debris that settles in our hearts blocks our healing. It can come in the form of limiting mindsets, unforgiveness, labels from others you just can't shake off, patterns and habits that keep you bound, or memories you just can't forget. Ask God to reveal to you the things your heart is holding that he wants to break you free from. Seek his truth and perspective for every area he reveals.

_____

_____

_____

_____

Allow God to Open My Heart to His View

My child you have been holding onto to things your heart was never meant to carry. Running away from the things you need to face has deepened the pain in your heart. You have come to believe things about yourself that just aren't true, and these thoughts cause you to protect yourself in ways that only add more pain to your life. I came so that you could be free, but your thoughts and actions continue to chain you. Fight for your freedom by letting go of the things that are holding you captive. Open your heart so that I can enter in. I want to give your heart a *reset!* Let me align the rhythm of your heartbeat with mine. Ba boom. Ba boom. Can you hear it? Can you feel it? The shock waves of my love and mercy are flowing through you now, shaking you free from the pain of the past. Freedom is pulsing through your veins. I'm calling your name. Run out of that grave into my glorious light!

Surrender to God's Way

In this time of prayer see your chains falling as you release to God what you were never meant to carry. Let the great heart surgeon take over. Picture your heart in his hands as he brings you back to life again and resets the rhythm of your heart. Watch as his perfect love washes away the pain, hurt, discouragement, fear, rejection, bitterness, and mistrust. Give God the space and time to expose the limiting mindsets (things you speak or believe) and protective strategies (things you do) that are hindering you from surrendering your heart to him and receiving the flow of his healing presence within. Break the power of any belief or strategy's hold over you by asking God to forgive you for partnering with views and actions that don't line up with his truth!

Write your own personal prayer of surrender here:

_____

_____

_____

_____

_____

_____

_____

_____

_____

_____

_____

Expect God to Move on My Behalf

Expect God's healing presence to set your heart free. Watch as it beats in a whole new way and thank him for the transformation happening within you.

Visualize a truth-filled thought based on what God revealed to your heart today and renew your mind in it all day long. Speak it, repeat it, be it!

My truth-focused thought for today:

_____

_____

Pause, Sit and Soak In His Presence

Sit and soak in the beauty of what God revealed to your heart today. Grant yourself the freedom to visualize fully and creatively express the thoughts, impressions, or images that come to your mind in any format that is best for you. Write, draw, paint, or collage allowing the images and words to flow freely from your heart so that your eyes can capture hope for the journey.

Mining Deeper

To mine is to dig deep and uncover treasures once hidden. It requires a search with the eyes and a heart that hungers for more. It is a willingness to explore unknown territory while trusting in the One leading the way. Over the course of the next few days, weeks, and months watch for how God continues to unfold deeper layers of truth regarding the area he spotlighted in your heart today. He rarely uncovers every layer all at once, because more than anything he wants daily intimacy with you. He wants you to mine the depths of his heart and as you do, he will uncover treasures before your eyes that will lead you to greater levels of freedom. Come back to this space to record and make note of the treasures he is leading your heart to discover!

Fill your thoughts with my words until they penetrate deep into your spirit. Then as you unwrap my words, they will impart true life and radiant health into the very core of your being.

Proverbs 4:21-22 (TPT)

Mining Topic: The place in my heart in need of God's view.

_____

My God-Directed Discoveries:

Day 29 Being Made New

Thought of the day: You are being made new!

I will CEASE today by choosing to:

Connect with God

Daily Word

Isaiah 43:19 (NLT)

For I am about to do something new. See, I have already begun! Do you not see it? I will make a pathway through the wilderness. I will create rivers in the dry wasteland.

Daily Worship

"There is A Cloud" by Elevation Worship

Note here how this verse and song spoke directly to your heart:

_____

_____

_____

_____

_____

_____

_____

Examine My Heart

Once you experience freedom, the enemy wants nothing more than to usher you right back into the places you were once chained. Speak back to your doubt and don't let discouragement cause you to jump off the path of transformation too quickly. Freedom is a process not an overnight task. Ask God to reveal any places of doubt within your heart. Let God grow in you the perseverance, determination, grit, courage, and trust you need to press on and move forward in your journey towards freedom.

_____

_____

_____

_____

Allow God to Open My Heart to His View

Open your arms and receive all the blessings I want to pour over you now! Feel them nourish your soul and empower you for the road of transformation ahead. Receive them! You are FREE! I am doing a new thing in you. You won't always understand it or be able to see the path clearly but trust that I am leading you in the right direction and that I will use everything for your good. My promises are true and full of power. Believe that my dreams for you will come to pass. I want to use you, bless you, and release you into your kingdom purpose. I will never leave you, but I will ask you to walk out onto waters that feel completely unstable. Hold my hand and let me stabilize you. This path I have for you will not be comfortable or easy, but I can guarantee my way is perfect. My heart is for you completely. Don't give back any ground to the enemy through doubt. Give me the time and space to make your transformation complete. Place your hope in me. I will see you through the wilderness. I will provide for your every need and lead you on the path I've designed for your life.

Surrender to God's Way

In this time of prayer let God fill your heart with courage and trust. Give God the space and time to expose any limiting mindsets (things you speak or believe) and protective strategies (things you do) that are attempting to keep you chained to the things God has already freed you from. Break the power of any belief or strategy's hold over you by asking God to forgive you for partnering with views and actions that don't line up with his truth!

Write your own personal prayer of surrender here:

_____

_____

_____

_____

_____

_____

_____

_____

_____

_____

_____

_____

_____

Expect God to Move on My Behalf

Expect that God's way is perfect, especially, when you are wading in the turbulent waters of transformation. He uses the unsettled waters to shake off you the things that would hinder you from moving forward in the plans he has for your life.

Visualize a truth-filled thought based on what God revealed to your heart today and renew your mind in it all day long. Speak it, repeat it, be it!

My truth-focused thought for today:

_____

_____

Pause, Sit and Soak In His Presence

Sit and soak in the beauty of what God revealed to your heart today. Grant yourself the freedom to visualize fully and creatively express the thoughts, impressions, or images that come to your mind in any format that is best for you. Write, draw, paint, or collage allowing the images and words to flow freely from your heart so that your eyes can capture hope for the journey.

Mining Deeper

To mine is to dig deep and uncover treasures once hidden. It requires a search with the eyes and a heart that hungers for more. It is a willingness to explore unknown territory while trusting in the One leading the way. Over the course of the next few days, weeks, and months watch for how God continues to unfold deeper layers of truth regarding the area he spotlighted in your heart today. He rarely uncovers every layer all at once, because more than anything he wants daily intimacy with you. He wants you to mine the depths of his heart and as you do, he will uncover treasures before your eyes that will lead you to greater levels of freedom. Come back to this space to record and make note of the treasures he is leading your heart to discover!

Fill your thoughts with my words until they penetrate deep into your spirit. Then as you unwrap my words, they will impart true life and radiant health into the very core of your being.

Proverbs 4:21-22 (TPT)

Mining Topic: The place in my heart in need of God's view.

_____

My God-Directed Discoveries:

_____

_____

_____

_____

_____

_____

_____

_____

_____

_____

_____

_____

_____

_____

_____

_____

Day 30 Preparing Your Heart for R.E.S.T

Thought of the day: Let your heart lead you into God's rest and presence for that is where he restores your soul.

I will CEASE today by choosing to:

Connect with God

Daily Word

Psalm 23:2–3 (TPT)

He offers a resting place for me in his luxurious love. His tracks take me to an oasis of peace, the quiet brook of bliss. That's where he restores and revives my life. He opens before me pathways to God's pleasure and leads me along in his footsteps of righteousness so that I can bring honor to his name.

Daily Worship

"Heart Abandoned" by Passion

Note here how this verse and song spoke directly to your heart:

_____

_____

_____

_____

_____

_____

_____

_____

Examine My Heart

Do you resist stillness? Has busyness become a form of protection—keeping you from looking within? Maybe busyness feels like significance to you. Are you stuck in a cycle of striving for God's promises, grace, and love when all he is asking you to do is rest in it? Ask God to reveal to your heart the things you are believing that keep you from entering his rest.

_____

_____

_____

Allow God to Open My Heart to His View

I want you to pause and meditate closely on the words that poured from David's heart above. They plot the course that leads to restoration and the plans I have made for you. Because of my great love for you, I created rest. I long to guide you to an oasis of peace far away from the distractions of life and beside still and quiet waters so that you can experience my heart and hear me whisper hope into your weary places. In the stillness is where your soul can be refreshed and restored. It is where I breathe life into the deadened places you never thought could be revived. Oh, the beautiful plans I have for you to enjoy. The path has already been carved by my grace and marked with your name. There is only one place you will discover it—only one place it is made visible. It will illuminate before you in the stillness of my presence. Come away with me and discover who you are meant to be!

Surrender to God's Way

In this time of prayer pause and still your heart and mind so that you can soak in the restorative power of God's presence. Give God the space and time to expose any limiting mindsets (things you speak or believe) and protective strategies (things you do) that are hindering you from entering his beautiful gift of rest. Break the power of any belief or strategy's hold over you by asking God to forgive you for partnering with views and actions that don't line up with his truth!

Write your own personal prayer of surrender here:

_____

_____

_____

_____

_____

_____

_____

_____

_____

_____

_____

_____

_____

_____

Expect God to Move on My Behalf

Expect God's rest to be your best strategy for success. You will never experience the immeasurably more God wants to accomplish through you without his presence.

Visualize a truth-filled thought based on what God revealed to your heart today and renew your mind in it all day long. Speak it, repeat it, be it!

My truth-focused thought for today:

_____

_____

Pause, Sit and Soak In His Presence

Sit and soak in the beauty of what God revealed to your heart today. Grant yourself the freedom to visualize fully and creatively express the thoughts, impressions, or images that come to your mind in any format that is best for you. Write, draw, paint, or collage allowing the images and words to flow freely from your heart so that your eyes can capture hope for the journey.

Mining Deeper

To mine is to dig deep and uncover treasures once hidden. It requires a search with the eyes and a heart that hungers for more. It is a willingness to explore unknown territory while trusting in the One leading the way. Over the course of the next few days, weeks, and months watch for how God continues to unfold deeper layers of truth regarding the area he spotlighted in your heart today. He rarely uncovers every layer all at once, because more than anything he wants daily intimacy with you. He wants you to mine the depths of his heart and as you do, he will uncover treasures before your eyes that will lead you to greater levels of freedom. Come back to this space to record and make note of the treasures he is leading your heart to discover!

Fill your thoughts with my words until they penetrate deep into your spirit. Then as you unwrap my words, they will impart true life and radiant health into the very core of your being.

Proverbs 4:21-22 (TPT)

Mining Topic: The place in my heart in need of God's view.

_____

My God-Directed Discoveries:

_____

_____

_____

_____

_____

_____

_____

_____

_____

_____

_____

_____

_____

_____

DAYS 31–37 Your Unique R.E.S.T Experience

It is time to practice the *art of the pause* for yourself. My hope for you is that this 40-day journey will not be just another experience that is easily forgotten, but truly a transformative time in your life where God's revelation and truth ignites a fire within you that cannot be contained and cannot be stopped! So, for the next seven days, I challenge you to fully submerge yourself into the flow of God's presence and learn to dance to the rhythm of his heartbeat. He has created the perfect vibration meant just for you. Trust that God knows how to speak directly to your heart and let him light the way to the freedom your soul has been longing for.

Here are a few verses to guide your unique R.E.S.T experience:

Mark 11:24 (MSG)

"...embrace this God-life, and you'll get God's everything."

Embrace God's way and he will not disappoint. You will be overwhelmed by what God wants to do in you and who he wants to be for you!

Exodus 33:13 (NLT)

"Let me know your ways so I may understand you more fully..."

Our sole focus is to understand God's way and his heart for us more fully for he alone holds the truth that set our hearts free!

Ephesians 2:10 (AMP)

"For we are His workmanship [His own master work, a work of art], created in Christ Jesus [reborn from above—spiritually transformed, renewed, ready to be used] for good works, which God prepared [for us] beforehand [taking paths which He set], so that we would walk in them [living the good life which He prearranged and made ready for us]."

He knows you completely and created you specifically for the pre-designed path your feet were meant to travel. Let him lead the way.

Day 31 Your Unique R.E.S.T Experience

You can use the format of CEASE or completely create your own as God guides your heart!

Thought of the day: God focus my heart and mind on what you want for me today. (Write the first thought that comes to your mind below.)

_____

_____

_____

I will CEASE today by choosing to:

Connect with God

Prepare your heart to hear God's heart. Pause here to worship and soak in God's Word.

Daily Word

_____

_____

Daily Worship

_____

_____

Examine My Heart

What am I holding in my heart, Lord, that needs your touch and perspective today?

_____

_____

_____

_____

_____

_____

_____

_____

_____

Allow God to Open My Heart to His View

Lord, what do you want my heart to know today? Help me to see through your eyes.

_____

_____

_____

_____

_____

_____

_____

_____

_____

_____

_____

Surrender to God's Way

God what are you asking me to surrender to you today?

_____

_____

_____

_____

_____

_____

_____

_____

_____

_____

_____

Expect God to Move on My Behalf

What do I need to trust you with today, Lord?

_____

_____

_____

_____

What is my truth-focused view for today?

_____

_____

_____

_____

Take note of how you are experiencing God in new and refreshing ways. Did you feel his presence in the lyrics of a song, or were you uplifted by an encouraging image, scripture verse, or message that spoke directly to your heart? Were you touched by the kindness of a friend, the hug of a loved one, or an experience in nature surrounded by his creation that pointed you right to him? Begin to see him all around you. His love notes are just waiting for you to open!

_____

_____

_____

_____

_____

_____

_____

_____

_____

_____

_____

Pause In His Presence and Mine His Heart...

Day 32 Your Unique R.E.S.T Experience

You can use the format of CEASE or completely create your own as God guides your heart!

Thought of the day: God focus my heart and mind on what you want for me today. (Write the first thought that comes to your mind below.)

_____

_____

_____

I will CEASE today by choosing to:

Connect with God

Prepare your heart to hear God's heart. Pause here to worship and soak in God's Word.

Daily Word

_____

_____

Daily Worship

_____

_____

Examine My Heart

What am I holding in my heart, Lord, that needs your touch and perspective today?

_____

_____

_____

_____

_____

_____

_____

_____

Allow God to Open My Heart to His View

Lord, what do you want my heart to know today? Help me to see through your eyes.

_____

_____

_____

_____

_____

_____

_____

_____

_____

_____

Surrender to God's Way

God what are you asking me to surrender to you today?

_____

_____

_____

_____

_____

_____

_____

_____

_____

_____

Expect God to Move on My Behalf

What do I need to trust you with today, Lord?

_____

_____

_____

_____

What is my truth-focused view for today?

_____

_____

_____

_____

Take note of how you are experiencing God in new and refreshing ways. Did you feel his presence in the lyrics of a song, or were you uplifted by an encouraging image, scripture verse, or message that spoke directly to your heart? Were you touched by the kindness of a friend, the hug of a loved one, or an experience in nature surrounded by his creation that pointed you right to him? Begin to see him all around you. His love notes are just waiting for you to open!

_____

_____

_____

_____

_____

_____

_____

_____

_____

_____

_____

_____

Pause In His Presence and Mine His Heart...

Day 33 Your Unique R.E.S.T Experience

You can use the format of CEASE or completely create your own as God guides your heart!

Thought of the day: God focus my heart and mind on what you want for me today. (Write the first thought that comes to your mind below.)

_____

_____

_____

I will CEASE today by choosing to:

Connect with God

Prepare your heart to hear God's heart. Pause here to worship and soak in God's Word.

Daily Word

_____

_____

Daily Worship

_____

_____

Examine My Heart

What am I holding in my heart, Lord, that needs your touch and perspective today?

_____

_____

_____

_____

_____

_____

_____

_____

Allow God to Open My Heart to His View

Lord, what do you want my heart to know today? Help me to see through your eyes.

_____

_____

_____

_____

_____

_____

_____

_____

_____

_____

_____

Surrender to God's Way

God what are you asking me to surrender to you today?

_____

_____

_____

_____

_____

_____

_____

_____

_____

_____

Expect God to Move on My Behalf

What do I need to trust you with today, Lord?

_____

_____

_____

_____

What is my truth-focused view for today?

_____

_____

_____

_____

Take note of how you are experiencing God in new and refreshing ways. Did you feel his presence in the lyrics of a song, or were you uplifted by an encouraging image, scripture verse, or message that spoke directly to your heart? Were you touched by the kindness of a friend, the hug of a loved one, or an experience in nature surrounded by his creation that pointed you right to him? Begin to see him all around you. His love notes are just waiting for you to open!

_____

_____

_____

_____

_____

_____

_____

_____

_____

_____

_____

_____

Pause In His Presence and Mine His Heart...

Day 34 Your Unique R.E.S.T Experience

You can use the format of CEASE or completely create your own as God guides your heart!

Thought of the day: God focus my heart and mind on what you want for me today. (Write the first thought that comes to your mind below.)

_____

_____

_____

I will CEASE today by choosing to:

Connect with God

Prepare your heart to hear God's heart. Pause here to worship and soak in God's Word.

Daily Word

_____

_____

Daily Worship

_____

_____

Examine My Heart

What am I holding in my heart, Lord, that needs your touch and perspective today?

_____

_____

_____

_____

_____

_____

_____

_____

Allow God to Open My Heart to His View

Lord, what do you want my heart to know today? Help me to see through your eyes.

_____

_____

_____

_____

_____

_____

_____

_____

_____

_____

Surrender to God's Way

God what are you asking me to surrender to you today?

_____

_____

_____

_____

_____

_____

_____

_____

_____

Expect God to Move on My Behalf

What do I need to trust you with today, Lord?

_____

_____

_____

_____

What is my truth-focused view for today?

_____

_____

_____

_____

Take note of how you are experiencing God in new and refreshing ways. Did you feel his presence in the lyrics of a song, or were you uplifted by an encouraging image, scripture verse, or message that spoke directly to your heart? Were you touched by the kindness of a friend, the hug of a loved one, or an experience in nature surrounded by his creation that pointed you right to him? Begin to see him all around you. His love notes are just waiting for you to open!

_____

_____

_____

_____

_____

_____

_____

_____

_____

_____

_____

_____

Pause In His Presence and Mine His Heart...

Day 35 Your Unique R.E.S.T Experience

You can use the format of CEASE or completely create your own as God guides your heart!

Thought of the day: God focus my heart and mind on what you want for me today. (Write the first thought that comes to your mind below.)

_____

_____

_____

I will CEASE today by choosing to:

Connect with God

Prepare your heart to hear God's heart. Pause here to worship and soak in God's Word.

Daily Word

_____

_____

Daily Worship

_____

_____

Examine My Heart

What am I holding in my heart, Lord, that needs your touch and perspective today?

_____

_____

_____

_____

_____

_____

_____

_____

_____

Allow God to Open My Heart to His View

Lord, what do you want my heart to know today? Help me to see through your eyes.

_____

_____

_____

_____

_____

_____

_____

_____

_____

_____

_____

_____

Surrender to God's Way

God what are you asking me to surrender to you today?

_____

_____

_____

_____

_____

_____

_____

_____

_____

_____

_____

Expect God to Move on My Behalf

What do I need to trust you with today, Lord?

_____

_____

_____

_____

What is my truth-focused view for today?

_____

_____

_____

_____

Take note of how you are experiencing God in new and refreshing ways. Did you feel his presence in the lyrics of a song, or were you uplifted by an encouraging image, scripture verse, or message that spoke directly to your heart? Were you touched by the kindness of a friend, the hug of a loved one, or an experience in nature surrounded by his creation that pointed you right to him? Begin to see him all around you. His love notes are just waiting for you to open!

_____

_____

_____

_____

_____

_____

_____

_____

_____

_____

_____

Pause In His Presence and Mine His Heart...

Day 36 Your Unique R.E.S.T Experience

You can use the format of CEASE or completely create your own as God guides your heart!

Thought of the day: God focus my heart and mind on what you want for me today. (Write the first thought that comes to your mind below.)

_____

_____

_____

I will CEASE today by choosing to:

Connect with God

Prepare your heart to hear God's heart. Pause here to worship and soak in God's Word.

Daily Word

_____

_____

Daily Worship

_____

_____

Examine My Heart

What am I holding in my heart, Lord, that needs your touch and perspective today?

_____

_____

_____

_____

_____

_____

_____

_____

Allow God to Open My Heart to His View

Lord, what do you want my heart to know today? Help me to see through your eyes.

_____

_____

_____

_____

_____

_____

_____

_____

_____

_____

Surrender to God's Way

God what are you asking me to surrender to you today?

_____

_____

_____

_____

_____

_____

_____

_____

_____

_____

Expect God to Move on My Behalf

What do I need to trust you with today, Lord?

_____

_____

_____

_____

What is my truth-focused view for today?

_____

_____

_____

_____

Take note of how you are experiencing God in new and refreshing ways. Did you feel his presence in the lyrics of a song, or were you uplifted by an encouraging image, scripture verse, or message that spoke directly to your heart? Were you touched by the kindness of a friend, the hug of a loved one, or an experience in nature surrounded by his creation that pointed you right to him? Begin to see him all around you. His love notes are just waiting for you to open!

_____

_____

_____

_____

_____

_____

_____

_____

_____

_____

_____

_____

Pause In His Presence and Mine His Heart...

Day 37 Your Unique R.E.S.T Experience

You can use the format of CEASE or completely create your own as God guides your heart!

Thought of the day: God focus my heart and mind on what you want for me today. (Write the first thought that comes to your mind below.)

_____

_____

_____

I will CEASE today by choosing to:

Connect with God

Prepare your heart to hear God's heart. Pause here to worship and soak in God's Word.

Daily Word

_____

_____

Daily Worship

_____

_____

Examine My Heart

What am I holding in my heart, Lord, that needs your touch and perspective today?

_____

_____

_____

_____

_____

_____

_____

_____

Allow God to Open My Heart to His View

Lord, what do you want my heart to know today? Help me to see through your eyes.

_____

_____

_____

_____

_____

_____

_____

_____

_____

_____

_____

Surrender to God's Way

God what are you asking me to surrender to you today?

_____

_____

_____

_____

_____

_____

_____

_____

_____

_____

Expect God to Move on My Behalf

What do I need to trust you with today, Lord?

_____

_____

_____

_____

What is my truth-focused view for today?

_____

_____

_____

_____

Take note of how you are experiencing God in new and refreshing ways. Did you feel his presence in the lyrics of a song, or were you uplifted by an encouraging image, scripture verse, or message that spoke directly to your heart? Were you touched by the kindness of a friend, the hug of a loved one, or an experience in nature surrounded by his creation that pointed you right to him? Begin to see him all around you. His love notes are just waiting for you to open!

_____

_____

_____

_____

_____

_____

_____

_____

_____

_____

_____

_____

Pause In His Presence and Mine His Heart...

Day 38 Reflections from R.E.S.T

Thought of the day: Rest is where God prepares you to be who he has called you to be.

I will CEASE today by choosing to:

Connect with God

Daily Word

John 7:38 (NLT)

Anyone who believes in me may come and drink! For the Scriptures declare, "Rivers of living water will flow from his heart."

Daily Worship

"In the River" by Jesus Culture

Note here how this verse and song spoke directly to your heart:

_____

_____

_____

_____

_____

_____

_____

_____

Examine My Heart

God's rest is where we experience the flow of his Spirit that makes us come alive in new ways. In what ways did your unique R.E.S.T experience bring life to your soul and dreams? In what places did you experience freedom and restoration? How has your view changed after seeking God's perspective?

_____

_____

_____

_____

_____

_____

Allow God to Open My Heart to His View

Rest is my nature. Peace flows from a heart that knows me and trusts in my way. I want you to see me all around you and know the inner workings of my heart. Develop a lifestyle of resting in me, and rivers of living water will flow freely from you. Do you feel it? Allow yourself to come alive in the River. I want to draw you close so that your heart will be full to the brim and overflowing with my Light. Open your heart daily to me so that I can continually pour restoration into your soul. Don't let anything settle in your heart that doesn't belong. I want nothing to hold you back from the plans I have for you. Rest in my truth, my love, and let me be the source of all your hope. Nothing can stop the joy that I place within you. I will spring up a well in you that cannot run dry. Rest in me so that my river of living water can continually flow in and through you and nourish your soul!

Surrender to God's Way

In this time of prayer spend time praising God and thanking him for the changes he is making in your heart and the freedom he is giving you. Let your words speak life to what he is doing in you and your praise burst open wide the river of his spirit flowing within you.

Write your own personal prayer of thankfulness here:

_____

_____

_____

_____

_____

_____

_____

_____

_____

_____

_____

_____

_____

_____

Expect God to Move on My Behalf

Expect God's rest to transform you and launch you forward into the plans he has for you. There is a river springing up in your heart and it cannot be stopped!

Visualize a truth-filled thought based on what God revealed to your heart today and renew your mind in it all day long. Speak it, repeat it, be it!

My truth-focused thought for today:

_____

_____

Pause, Sit and Soak In His Presence

Sit and soak in the beauty of what God revealed to your heart today. Grant yourself the freedom to visualize fully and creatively express the thoughts, impressions, or images that come to your mind in any format that is best for you. Write, draw, paint, or collage allowing the images and words to flow freely from your heart so that your eyes can capture hope for the journey.

Mining Deeper

To mine is to dig deep and uncover treasures once hidden. It requires a search with the eyes and a heart that hungers for more. It is a willingness to explore unknown territory while trusting in the One leading the way. Over the course of the next few days, weeks, and months watch for how God continues to unfold deeper layers of truth regarding the area he spotlighted in your heart today. He rarely uncovers every layer all at once, because more than anything he wants daily intimacy with you. He wants you to mine the depths of his heart and as you do, he will uncover treasures before your eyes that will lead you to greater levels of freedom. Come back to this space to record and make note of the treasures he is leading your heart to discover!

Fill your thoughts with my words until they penetrate deep into your spirit. Then as you unwrap my words, they will impart true life and radiant health into the very core of your being.

Proverbs 4:21-22 (TPT)

Mining Topic: The place in my heart in need of God's view.

_____

My God-Directed Discoveries:

_____

_____

_____

_____

_____

_____

_____

_____

_____

_____

_____

_____

_____

Day 39 The Light Inside You

Thought of the day: You were created to SHINE! Experience Freedom by living out your purpose.

I will CEASE today by choosing to:

Connect with God

Daily Word

Matthew 5:14–15 (MSG)

You're here to be light, bringing out the God-colors in the world. God is not a secret to be kept. We're going public with this, as public as a city on a hill. If I make you light-bearers, you don't think I'm going to hide you under a bucket, do you? I'm putting you on a light stand. Now that I've put you there on a hilltop, on a light stand—shine.

Daily Worship

"The Comeback" by Danny Gokey

Note here how this verse and song spoke directly to your heart:

_____

_____

_____

_____

_____

_____

_____

Examine My Heart

Get to know the light God has placed inside you. Ask God to show you the passion burning in your heart and where he wants you to shine your light for him.

_____

_____

_____

_____

_____

Allow God to Open My Heart to His View

There is a passion, a fire rising in you. This is your time. You are learning how to surrender to me and lay yourself down at my feet. I have been waiting for this day—this moment where you would embrace the beauty I have placed inside you. Thank you for trusting me with your heart. Now I can speak life into the dreams I have designed just for you. I want to share "You" with my world. There are people that are longing for the light you were created to give away. I can't wait to see you walking in the truth of who you are and no longer letting your past rob you of all you were meant to be. You were made for more! Let my truth plant your feet on the path I have for you. Don't quit. Stay the course. I promise it will all be worth it!

Surrender to God's Way

In this time of prayer picture God placing his light inside you and see yourself sharing it with the world. Imagine the impact you will have as your embrace who you are in Christ and trust in his power at work within you! Give God the space and time to expose any limiting mindsets (things you speak or believe) and protective strategies (things you do) that are hindering you from boldly shining your light. Break the power of any belief or strategy's hold over you by asking God to forgive you for partnering with views and actions that don't line up with his truth!

Write your own personal prayer of surrender here:

_____

_____

_____

_____

_____

_____

_____

_____

_____

_____

_____

_____

_____

_____

Expect God to Move on My Behalf

Expect God to empower you to do whatever he has designed you for. Don't let anything hold you back. You were created to SHINE and be a light for all to see!

Visualize a truth-filled thought based on what God revealed to your heart today and renew your mind in it all day long. Speak it, repeat it, be it!

My truth-focused thought for today:

_____

_____

Pause, Sit and Soak In His Presence

Sit and soak in the beauty of what God revealed to your heart today. Grant yourself the freedom to visualize fully and creatively express the thoughts, impressions, or images that come to your mind in any format that is best for you. Write, draw, paint, or collage allowing the images and words to flow freely from your heart so that your eyes can capture hope for the journey.

Mining Deeper

To mine is to dig deep and uncover treasures once hidden. It requires a search with the eyes and a heart that hungers for more. It is a willingness to explore unknown territory while trusting in the One leading the way. Over the course of the next few days, weeks, and months watch for how God continues to unfold deeper layers of truth regarding the area he spotlighted in your heart today. He rarely uncovers every layer all at once, because more than anything he wants daily intimacy with you. He wants you to mine the depths of his heart and as you do, he will uncover treasures before your eyes that will lead you to greater levels of freedom. Come back to this space to record and make note of the treasures he is leading your heart to discover!

Fill your thoughts with my words until they penetrate deep into your spirit. Then as you unwrap my words, they will impart true life and radiant health into the very core of your being.

Proverbs 4:21-22 (TPT)

Mining Topic: The place in my heart in need of God's view.

_____

My God-Directed Discoveries:

_____

_____

_____

_____

_____

_____

_____

_____

_____

_____

_____

_____

_____

_____

_____

Day 40 Share Your Story

Thought of the day: Your life is a letter that will encourage others to experience freedom!

I will CEASE today by choosing to:

Connect with God

Daily Word

John 8:36 (NLT)

So if the Son set you free, you are truly free.

2 Corinthians 3:3 (MSG)

Your very lives are a letter that anyone can read by just looking at you. Christ himself wrote it—not with ink, but with God's living Spirit; not chiseled into stone, but carved into human lives—and we publish it.

Daily Worship

"Look How He Lifted Me" by Elevation Worship

Note here how this verse and song spoke directly to your heart:

_____

_____

_____

_____

_____

_____

_____

Examine My Heart

Now that your heart has received new revelation, new actions are required. What is God asking you to do differently moving forward and what is he wanting you to share with his world?

_____

_____

_____

_____

Allow God to Open My Heart to His View

No one can be you. I will use your story to be a light that leads others to freedom. Nothing in your past disqualifies you from being used by me. I waste nothing. Your experience has shaped you for such a time as this. Allow this encounter with me to spark a fire in you that cannot be stopped. Believe in the freedom your heart has experienced and walk confidently in who you are in me! Stop all lies from entering your heart regarding your destiny and future. Any thought that limits you is not from me! I have a hope-filled, mountain-moving spirit for you to possess. Rebuild your life on my truth, always reframing your perspective with my Word and nothing will hinder your progress. You were made for such a time as this! There is NOTHING we can't do together! Give me all of your heart and in return you will be able to experience all of mine!

Surrender to God's Way

In this time of prayer seek God's next move for your life. Live boldly for him. Let him speak directly to your heart about what he is calling you to do in this moment. Don't let anything hold you back from being the light he has created you to be. Ask him to light the way before you and trust that he will never leave you, forsake you, or withhold anything that you need for the journey ahead of you.

Write your freedom declaration here. "I am free to be... "

_____

_____

_____

_____

_____

_____

_____

_____

_____

_____

_____

_____

_____

_____

_____

Expect God to Move on My Behalf

Expect that God's vision will always come with his provision! Let your heart spill over with thankfulness as you praise him for the freedom he has poured into you. May your new walk reveal the freed person you are!

Visualize a truth-filled thought based on what God revealed to your heart today and renew your mind in it all day long. Speak it, repeat it, be it!

My truth-focused thought for today:

_____

_____

Pause, Sit, and Soak In His Presence

Sit and soak in the beauty of what God revealed to your heart over these last 40 days. What was the overwhelming message you heard from God's heart to yours? Grant yourself the freedom to creatively express how this experience has impacted you!

Mining Deeper

To mine is to dig deep and uncover treasures once hidden. It requires a search with the eyes and a heart that hungers for more. It is a willingness to explore unknown territory while trusting in the One leading the way. Over the course of the next few days, weeks, and months watch for how God continues to unfold deeper layers of truth regarding the area he spotlighted in your heart today. He rarely uncovers every layer all at once, because more than anything he wants daily intimacy with you. He wants you to mine the depths of his heart and as you do, he will uncover treasures before your eyes that will lead you to greater levels of freedom. Come back to this space to record and make note of the treasures he is leading your heart to discover!

Fill your thoughts with my words until they penetrate deep into your spirit. Then as you unwrap my words, they will impart true life and radiant health into the very core of your being.

Proverbs 4:21-22 (TPT)

Mining Topic: The place in my heart in need of God's view.

My God-Directed Discoveries:

Appendix

Next Steps—Join the 40-Day Journey Community

Thank you for taking part in *The 40-Day Journey*. I am believing that God will complete in you what he has begun and that you will continue to experience more and more levels of freedom in your life. As a next step, we would love for you to share your 40-day experience with us and let your life be a letter that encourages someone else on their journey to freedom! Join our community of overcomers at shinehealing.org and click the "connect" tab to share your story! I've included a space below to get you started!

We would also love for you to connect with us in person by participating in one of our Freedom 23 Experiences. Come away to Selah Ranch for an encounter like no other. We offer four programs to meet a variety of needs: Women's Retreats & Individual Self-Discovery Experiences, Family-Building Groups, and Ministry Team Building Days. We want to help women, families, and ministry leaders rest, reset, and run their race for Christ. We believe that purpose is birthed from and revived by stillness in God's presence. There is no greater example of restorative rest ever described than what David paints for us in Psalm 23. Our goal is to create a unique, faith-building Psalm's 23 experience where God can restore and refresh your heart and lead you on the path he has designed for you, your family, or your ministry. Check out our website for more detailed information and to sign up for one of our "Freedom 23" experiences.

Finally, follow us on Facebook, Instagram #theshinementality, and our blog for a regular dose of encouragement!

Be Bold—Be a Light!

40-Day Reflection—Write Your Story

Reflect on your experience over the last 40 days. Record it so you can share it and pass on the blessing. Let your experience and testimony bring light and hope to others.

Take note of the ways you Encountered God, Discovered You, and Experienced Freedom during these last 40 days! In what ways do you see yourself, God, and your future differently now?

_____

_____

_____

_____

_____

_____

_____

_____

Weekly Emotions Journal

Identify the top 3 feelings you had each day, write each feeling in a color on the lines provided. Then fill in the heart with the colors that represent each feeling you experienced.

Copyright © 2018 by Shine Healing Ministries

What has been the overall emotional picture of my heart this week?

_____

_____

_____

Copyright © 2018 by Shine Healing Ministries

Common Negative Limiting Mindsets and Protective Strategies

Negative Limiting Mindsets

I am not good enough
It's not ok to show/feel my emotions
I don't matter
I am not loveable
I am all alone
I am worthless
I can't trust myself
I am inadequate
I deserve bad things
I am damaged/broken
I am powerless
I am not safe
I'm unworthy of care
I'll never get better
I am flawed
It's all my fault
People always leave
I can't depend on others
I don't deserve love
I am weak
I am insignificant
I am a failure
I am not in control
I am a nobody
I don't belong
Nobody cares
I am a burden
I have no purpose
I don't deserve to live
_____
_____

Protective Strategies

Perfectionism & Seeking Accomplishments
Passive-Aggressive Actions or Manipulation
Accept Abusive Treatment
Closed Heart—Don't Let Anyone In
Self-Reliance/Never Ask for Help
Rage—Use Anger to Keep People at a Distance
Procrastinate or Indecisive
Judgmental and Extra Critical of Others
Self-Harm (cutting/eating d/o)
Hopelessness
Depression
Isolate
People Please
Suicidal Thoughts/Attempts
Shut down/Dissociate
Faking Happy-Mask Wearer
Seek to Control Everything/Everyone
Avoidance/Minimization/Denial
Abuse Substances
Promiscuity
Deny Own Needs-Excessive Caregiving
Panic, Worry, Think the Worst
Self-Sabotage or Sabotage Relationships
Withdraw through Social Media/TV
Excessive Spending or Hoarding
Push Emotions Down/Numb Out
Create Conflict/Fight/Create Drama
Self-Critical/Self-Hate
Accepting False Responsibility
_____ (Fill in your own.)
_____ (Fill in your own.)

Circle the mindsets that feel true for you and then draw a line to the protective strategy that corresponds with how you tend to react when you trust this belief.

Copyright © 2018 by Shine Healing Ministries

Encouragement for the Road Ahead

We all know the excitement can fade after a powerful experience, and life just picks back up again. So, I wanted to provide you with freedom reminders to fill your heart with hope and inspire the fire God has placed within you to keep burning. Use the phrases provided (or create a few of your own) to interrupt the intrusion of limiting beliefs in your heart that no longer belong! You are Free!

Freedom Reminders

- The Mountain Mover Lives In Me

- The Light Within Me Is Unstoppable

- I Am Always Enough In Christ

- Nothing Can Disqualify Me from Being Used by God

- I Am Free To Run With My Dreams

- God Wants To Share "Me" With His World

- God Made No Mistakes When He Designed My Heart

- I Am SO Worth It

- Healing Is a Process—I Won't Quit Before My Miracle Happens

- Freedom Is Mine To Receive

- It's My Time To SHINE

Create your own here:

_____

_____

_____

About the Author

Josie is a speaker, author, professional clinical counselor, and advocate for all the light-bearers out there who have yet to discover how brightly they can shine! In her work with people who have felt lost, damaged, and not enough, she has witnessed their struggle to hope again, and it has molded her passion to become an outspoken voice for those who are held back by their past. She believes that one of the biggest challenges to overcoming the obstacles we face is awareness. "We don't know what we don't know." Therefore, she is passionate about helping others discover what is blocking their progress and encouraging them to move forward in their God-given purpose.

Josie is the founder of Shine Healing Ministries and author of Shining Freely. She and her husband, Nathan's, newest endeavor is the creation of Selah Ranch. A creative oasis and retreat center far away from distractions, designed to usher people into God's presence and bring back the "Art of the Pause".

Josie enjoys speaking, writing, and unlocking the flow of creativity in every human heart. She is learning how to ride the roller coaster of being a momma to two tween-girls, loves Jesus, and can't get enough of soaking in the natural beauty all around her.

Notes...

for all your newly acquire Bright Ideas!

for all your newly acquire Bright Ideas!

Made in the
USA
Lexington, KY

54563426R00131